PILGRIM

LIVING YOUR YOGA EVERY SINGLE DAY

PILGRIM

This is who I am.
Beneath masks and hats and history.
I am whole. Holy.
Enough as is.
And when this voice from deep within comes forth and speaks of
Truth, There is a knowing that bubbles, rises, and reveals each day,
Each moment as choice, not chore.
This revelation is laced with potential, possibility.
Illuminating me as Pilgrim. Pilgrim of light.
Shedding rays of curiosity and willingness to see
through the darkness,
to see into the likes of confusion, loss or sideway emotion.
To gracefully, softly, hold myself in sacred conversation.
And so I journey.
I journey inward, past the right and wrong of it, past the
illusion of limitation.
I know, in this limited body that I am *not* that.
For I am That.
All THAT.
And I know how to shine this mirror.
Pan for this gold. Mine this preciousness.
I know that all that wants to live through me must come through
the temple doors. I know that my offering, my service, my light,
shines through me from a source of brilliance much greater
than my softly lit imaginings.
And I know better than to exorcise the demons,
For the risk of driving out the angels is much too great to bear in
one holy life. I walk barefoot, toes spread, soul upon this earth,
touching and being
the healer, the healed, the healing.
The breath, the breather, the one being breathed.
I stand in this body tall, rooted, upward reaching,
Blooming forth and bestowing flower,
Then fruit, then seed to soil.
I am divine abalone dream
Turning head & catching breath.
I laugh. Oh, how I laugh,
As I source my body, my bones, my blood as bread, as dancer,
As slave for to all who want a slave.
I need not tell you, but I will,
That this whisper come from a source beyond, a voice beyond,
extraterrestrial, intracellular.
And I hear you.
I see you
I am you
And I thank you

PILGRIM

LIVING YOUR YOGA EVERY SINGLE DAY

Britt B Steele

BrittBSteele.com

Deva Daaru YogaFarm
2016

Published by Deva Daaru c/o Britt B Steele
P.O. Box 372
Vernonia, OR 97064

ISBN-13:
978-1534867079
ISBN-10:
1534867074

Printed in the United Sates of America

SECOND EDITION

Table of Contents

Words From The Author
From the Hills of India

Words From The Author

How do I offer gratitude for what has become a part of me or what may have never actually been separate from me? There is no one experience nor person that has come into my life and serves as the cause of all this. Instead, it has been a conglomeration of magic, light, and love. To all of you, I am grateful beyond words.

I learned from my beloved teacher that the real teacher is neither person nor personality. The real teacher is the teaching itself. And yet, I stand beneath the flow of clarity and knowledge and drink from the waters of Truth that come as a result of my teacher's dedication and his willingness to do his personal work and to surrender his ego again and again. I trust him as a pure and guiding light, and if or when his clear presence falls away, I will have the teachings as my guru.

I thank Yoga for this, for my primary teacher, for so many other teachers who have come and gone and come again, and for my own body-mind complex for being my humble and formidable escort this time around.

I also offer this book to my sweet husband, best friend, and soul partner on this pilgrimage. Without your light, these gifts would not be seen nor expressed in this life. You are my rock and my reason: My heart is devoted to you.

Further, I offer this book to all of the brilliant lights who have taken a pilgrimage before me, struggled, and doubted, who have been ostracized, criticized, judged, or maimed for speaking Truth. And I offer this book to all of the "little lamps" who question their own light, potential, purpose, or abilities. You are as brilliant as anyone I have ever known, and it is my greatest desire that you see your radiance shining forth upon your path with each prayerful, purposeful step.

This little light of mine,
I'm gonna let it shine.
Let it shine. Let it shine. Let it shine.

From the Hills of India

By Dr. Deborah Kern

... As I sit here overlooking the Nilgiri forests at an Ayurvedic clinic in Southern India, I am awestruck by living Ayurveda leaping from the pages of this sacred yet accessible text. If ever there were a book that was written from the inside out, this is it.

I've been blessed to know and love Britt for over 20 years. We've both followed a path of yoga and Ayurveda, and I've witnessed Britt dive deep, throwing herself fully into the study and practice and coming out a bright and shining example of truly living her Yoga.

I have never known a yoga teacher who lives her yoga— in the modern world —more than Britt. She provides a rigor and freedom in her teaching that comes only from someone who is following a lineage and dedicated to the rare and true teachings of Yoga.

This book is a reflection of Britt. It is beautiful, deep, sacred, practical, inspired, and inspiring. I so appreciate the way Britt stays true to the Yogic teachings while making them accessible to a modern-day householder. Because she has integrated the ancient principles of Ayurveda into her own life, she explains esoteric spiritual concepts in a way that anyone can grasp—and then she guides you with practices to apply and integrate these concepts into your life.

Whether you're new to yoga and Ayurveda or have a long-standing practice, may this book be a blessing in your life as it has been in mine.

Dr. Deborah Kern
MBA, PhD, YTT500
devoted mother, author, and women's wellness empowerment guide

Dedicated to all Truth seekers

Introduction

What does it mean to be a Pilgrim?

To be a pilgrim is to set forth on a spiritual journey with a holy destination in mind. It is accompanied by a willingness to fully experience whatever is necessary to reach one's destination. If you have ever gone to your yoga practice in search of something more than the physical benefits of the practice, you know what I mean in your bones. Whether you have practiced a lot of yoga, dabbled in it, or have yet to unroll a yoga mat, I say: You are a Yogi, not because you do (or do not) have a regular yoga practice, but because you know what it feels like to be out of sync, and you know what it feels like to be in sync—and the "in sync" state is what you seek—in every cell in your body you seek this. We call this state homeostasis—universal harmony, a symbiosis with all that is—and this state is the true state of Yoga.

The following pages outline a mighty pilgrimage. Already, you have taken the first steps toward what can evolve into a most sacred journey, with opportunities to discover hidden treasures and to meet other journeyers along the way. This book serves as your map and your guidebook.

I have been a pilgrim a very long time.

The vision I have for you on this pilgrimage comes from my own journey. I've wandered this whole life. Even while maintaining the duties of a householder, student, wife, and career woman, I have constantly wandered, mostly alone—or so I have thought. I have always felt a little "different." It isn't my style to take life lightly. I have often felt like I live in two worlds: one full of stuff to do, produce, and prove, and another where I am totally at peace with myself, even if I have nothing, do nothing, and achieve nothing. Having been on many pilgrimages, I know that those of us who walk this path don't really choose it. It chooses us. (I'm not saying there aren't choices, but I will get to that later.) Walking a spiritual path comes when we see the sacred in all things, when we are looking for ways to raise ourselves up and to fill our lives with "higher" things so that which no longer serves us might easily fall away without effort or loss. This is the power that comes naturally to the pilgrim.

As we see the sacred, we also see that all things are in right order, and we begin to recognize fullness in all things at all times. As this happens, we realize how this fullness presents as potential within everyone, and we realize our power to heal our own bodies, minds, hearts, and spirits. For most, this potential lies dormant throughout one's entire life, much like the portions of the brain that are never called upon to awaken and serve up their power. When we activate this potential, we not only awaken each day with a zest to offer ourselves freely and joyfully to all that comes our way, we also satiate a hungry world that awaits the sharing of our consciousness and our greatest, most impressive gifts.

This Pilgrimage is sacred.

My desire is for you to give up all limited thinking, to take each moment into your heart, and to abandon all urges to call anything good or bad, black or white, right or wrong, enough or not enough. Instead, stand in the "sacred gray" and drop all offense/ defense posturing and receive wholeheartedly this one holy life as it is: right here, right now, all right.

This book is your map and guide to help you navigate your way. It is the blessing of circumstances that has led you to this moment and to this particular point on your journey. You may have stood and looked out from your life from a similar point, a new experience, program, or embarkment, but you have certainly never before stood here, exactly as you are, in this moment. Not ever. It may feel familiar, but I guarantee that it is different. You are different. Nothing is the same. And everything is here. Now, if you stand very still in this place, you will feel something: that what you are seeking on this journey is seeking you.

It's important to note at the beginning of this journey that this is not a religious-based personal journey. I offer this as a spiritual journey that allows but does not require you to bring with you a "religious" disposition. Ultimately, yoga is not religious. If there is any religion, if you will, associated with Yoga as a whole, it is the religion of love, and love welcomes all.

Everything I offer through these pages I invite you to receive and allow to wash over your life, exactly as it is. In its essence, nothing that I say is in conflict with your chosen tradition or belief system. You can take what serves you and let all else go without hanging on to anything that doesn't serve your highest good or feel right.

I am grateful to walk with you. To narrow the chasm between where the edges of your world fade out and the edges of my world fade in. This is the essence of Yoga with a capital Y—the big union where we come together and know deep down that we are so much more similar to one other than we are different. I am the world and the world is me. Yoga with a capital Y refers to all of the practices beyond the mat—all of the touchstones I'm going to share with you and anything and everything that leads us to a deeper understanding that we are connected to everything—while yoga with a small y refers to the asanas (poses) on the mat.

Let's walk. Shall we?

You are a seeker. Always have been. A little different, maybe. And I bet you even feel a little lonely sometimes. This is good news.

In ancient times it was believed that our mere longing was the answer to our prayers. It is the longing that reminds us to reach for more—something greater than ourselves. It is the longing that encourages us to keep moving forward, walking a spiritual path, a sometimes delightful, and other times arduous, path toward our own brilliance.

The only problem with this is that in modern times there is so much noise, so many demands, requests, responsibilities, and opportunities that keep pulling us into the woods. So instead of enjoying the simplicity and ease of a well-worn soul's path, we find ourselves looking for fulfillment in places and spaces where it simply cannot be found. Where we can never be fulfilled. And this pointless search leaves us feeling alone, exhausted, and lonely. This is also good news—for in the longing, the seeking, the journey itself, are the answers we have always been longing to hear. And you, Dear One, have taken the first steps on an amazing path—a path that I know, firsthand, results in peace and ease of heart. This path is circle—a circle of your own life. It ends at the beginning, where we are intimately interconnected to all things, and where we realize how simple and full this life can be.

Navigate Your Way.

Live Your Yoga: Over the course of this journey, you will find that living your Yoga, that integration and finding connection between and among all things and experiences, will shorten the distance between "What?" and "So what?" or "So what now?" in your life. This is one of the most profound measures of how we take what we learn cognitively and infuse it into every morsel of our being.

You Already Are: You are already everything that you seek on this journey, everything you're longing for, everything you desire. Everything you want to shed is not you; it never was. Everything that you're holding on to or that is holding you is not you. Everything that you dream of becoming is already here within you. This is the siddhi (blessing) of the pilgrimage.

Walk Your Own Path: This is one path—not the only path, but the path that has proven itself to me and revealed unfathomable brilliance in my life. I've seen its power when I received a phone call reminding me that life is precious. I've seen its grace when loss knocked on my door. I've seen its resilience when I've been in an automobile accident. In all of these moments, I have seen how walking this path has given me more than I imagined possible.

The More You Give, the More You Receive: Here is how I see it: The more that you are able to step into this and the more that you tap into this every single day, the more that these practices will bless you.

The Time Is Now Because You Are Here: Take pause when you are touched deeply. Lean into what supports you. Ready or not, it makes no difference. Take one single sacred step. Your life is waiting for you.

The First Steps.

The first steps are not physical in nature. They are cognitive shifts, pondering and preparation that will lay a foundation for you to take this journey in ease and clarity.

Prepare yourself:

Life just keeps coming. Whether you are ready or not. Time passes, and takes with it all that we've offered up to each precious moment. You can do every moment just as you always have and create a bunch more of what you've got, and that is all right. Or, you can prepare yourself for the journey ahead: Close your eyes, sense that there is more, and that this "more-ness" comes from a place deep within you—not out of lack or need or the longing to become something different, but instead from a place of abundance, overflow, wholeness, holy wonder, and a fullness yet unrealized.

Free your mind:

Freeing the mind is a must on this journey. Relax the heart, soften the breath, and allow each exhale to release what you do not need at any given point on the journey and each inhale to fill you with what serves you best. The journey within is most delicious when we feel free… free to explore the side roads, free to stop and take in all that we are experiencing through our senses. As you take these steps, here are a few ways to make this an even more extraordinary adventure.

Reserve time and space:

It may sound funny, but finding a perfect time of day, for just that perfect amount of time, in a perfect location, to take these practices to heart is the foundation of your journey. I might suggest morning, especially before the rest of your house has roused, as that is when your mind is the most fresh and simultaneously sharp. Early morning is particularly suited to living one's Yoga and is often referred to as the "hour of ambrosia"—the time before sunrise is a transformative time when the light of the day joins with the light of our own consciousness. This is a potent and quiet time. It naturally provides a gateway to align the energies and intentions of your body with the energies and intentions of the universe. Classically, this time is 48 minutes before the sun rises. If you're up for that as your designated time and space, I say, all the more power to you (literally). And if not, I say fitting it in somewhere, anywhere, is better than not. As far as length of time you set aside, 30 minutes is a suitable aspiration. However, if you have 10 minutes at best, then take 10 with reverence. As far as location, you can determine a spot that serves you best, where you may have some privacy and are in a pleasant setting. Dedicating yourself to these practices in this way offers a conscious commitment that is the foundation of any and all lasting transformation. It simply needs to be comfortable and feel suitable. Nothing fancy, just functional. The sweetness you bring to this time and place will sweeten the space.

Fast from technology:

This is important—just as a pilgrim does not go backwards between steps, it is most beneficial for you to commit your space and time to staying on the path of the pilgrimage. This is the best time to turn off your cell phone and computer and put them in another room. This is the time to create a natural space for yourself with no unnecessary distractions, even music. Imagine doing this practice 100 years ago and create an environment that could have been replicated back then. The silence and natural environment allows you to see the portal and to go through it.

Settle in:
Get comfy, grab a cup of your favorite tea or hot water with a wedge of lime, settle in on the couch, or build yourself a nest on your yoga mat. Remind the family or housemates that you would like some uninterrupted time. Make an agreement that you are to be summoned only if there is an emergency. If anyone needs something or calls, they should write it down and you'll get to it when you are finished.

Start and be where you are:
This is not a journey that requires a start date and an end date. In fact, that may hinder the depth and meaning of this journey. Take the time you need and allow the process to guide you. There is no formula for completing this journey. You may find you want to spend 4–5 days on one touchstone, delving in, journaling, making plans for bringing it more brilliantly into your life and practices. There may be some touchstones that take very little time to feel complete. The whole process might take you a week, or it might evolve into months—that part is up to you. Go as deeply as you are willing, with no rush to get on to the next exercise or the next touchstone. It is the process that marks your success, not the completion of the process.

Study yourself:
In the Yogic tradition, we speak about svadhyaya (self-study). This means taking a deep, true, and non-judgmental look at our lives and standing in the "sacred gray" as we do our very best not to make what we find "right" or "wrong." This entire journey is about slowing down, seeing yourself, sensing the integration and the points of dis-integration. Then, it is about reconnecting the aspects of your physical, mental, emotional, and spiritual life that were once whole and have somehow separated.

Stalk truth:
In all of this, we are on the lookout for Truth—with a capital T. This isn't the "truth" that is relative and requires a comparison, such as "I am tired" (compared to when I was young), or "I am strong" (compared to when I didn't practice yoga). But instead Truth is what remains, in its absolute way, when everything else

10

falls away. It is the ultimate Yoga—where all things come from fullness, exist in fullness, and return to fullness. It is the commonality between all spiritual paths, seekers, traditions, and lovers. It is light, not heat. It is undeniable, indescribable, unjustifiable, and whole. Truth cannot be categorized, "proven," or "disproven." It is what remains when everything else that is not Truth falls away. Simply holding space for this, as one holds a sacred stone in their pocket on a journey to remind them of holy purpose, is all this pilgrimage asks of you.

In doing just this, Truth shall arise and Truth shall remain.

And it all starts within.

The Twelve Touchstones

This book is a holy lamp, and this is a sacred journey.

Pilgrim is designed to offer you light and vision unto yourself, one prayerful moment, one simple and true practice, at a time. This book has 12 unique yet interconnected touchstones, each with their own exercises designed to unfold your inner wisdom and Truth.

What is a touchstone?
Originally, a touchstone was a gray or black fine-grained stone to which precious metals were "touched" (or rubbed) to see if a trace of the precious metal was left behind. This trace established the validity of the metal. (Of course the metal really needed no validating; it only needed to be deemed valid in the limited eyes of the beholder.) In this same way, and in this circumstance, you are what is precious, and these touchstones are the inert flint on which your precious composition is revealed. As a result of practicing these touchstones, your true and immutable nature will be extracted and shine brilliantly through—to your own eyes.

Upon seeing your own beauty, recognizing that you are precious and fine in and through, you begin to recognize your true nature and therefore move forth in your life in your sacred purpose, with this knowing of perfection and wholeness as your foundation. And I am here to tell you, knowing this makes all the difference in how you show up in your life and on this planet.

Working with the Touchstones
As you move through the touchstones, you will find activities and exercises woven into the text. Ponder these, journal about these, or explore them to the depth that suits you.

At the end of each touchstone you will find "one simple practice," which is exactly that: a practice of body, mind, or heart that is available for you to deepen your understanding and assimilation of the touchstone. Again, ponder these, journal about these, or explore these simple practices and watch how the touchstone itself touches you. The ancient Yogic teachings tell us that

14

Yoga will bless us a thousandfold in return for whatever it is we give to the practice. Just imagine how much blessing can come your way by living your Yoga, every single day.

Touchstone #1: Move My Body

This isn't your regular yoga book.

Why not? Because I don't see yoga as "exercise". In fact, I don't believe in exercise. Not anymore. I used to walk and run and lift weights and teach these boot camp–style fitness classes. I am so over that.

Now, I move the way my body naturally. The way it was intended to move. And even though in the last decade or so I've changed the way I move, I didn't blow up fat. I didn't lose all my muscle mass. But I did lean down. My posture has improved. And my aches and pains, although I'm not claiming to be enlightened of my suffering, have diminished exponentially.

These days, I use movement to inspire me, and to open clogged channels in my body so prana (universal life force) can effortlessly pulse through my body. More importantly, I use movement to stimulate juiciness and freedom in my whole life. No more thinking about burning calories, reaching my target heart rate, or counting down the time on the treadmill. No more counting. It is vitality that counts. And it is balance, joy, ease, health, and sustainable practices that I seek.

You can call this wellness if you want. I know it in my bones as Yoga with the big Y. Yoga isn't something that you do only on the mat. It is something that you are—beneath all the hubbub of busy, too much of a good thing and not enough of another, Yoga with the big Y is what we are when everything we do is aligned with what we want to be doing, the vision of ourselves we long to present, and the higher purpose for our being here.

What does it mean to "live one's yoga"?

It looks like a daily asana practice… some days challenging, some days more gentle, some days healing, some days still. Upside down, twisting, breathing, flowing, feeling, stilling, distilling. Every practice has an intention, a heartfelt sankalpa (daily resolution) that you set at the beginning of your time on the mat. The practice can be 10 minutes, an hour and 10 minutes, or more. It is where your mat becomes your magic carpet, carrying you to dreamy places. Your asana practice, along with pranayama (breath practices designed to affect energy patterns) and spending time in the hands of nature, is one of the best ways to keep your body strong, clear, infused with life force, and ready for anything. It's good stuff. For me, my asana practice is "coming home."

Okay, so you say to yourself, "I don't feel 'at home' when I get to the mat." Maybe you don't even own a yoga mat. I say this: If you would have come to the place you live now two years before it was yours and pulled up, parked, and stood outside the front door, you would not have recognized it as your "home." It might have been nice. Or maybe it wouldn't have been your style. But now, having made it your own day after day, month after month, year after year, you recognize it as your "home." It's the same with yoga. The first time I went to the mat, I was all about getting through the practice. My shoulders were achy. My wrists hurt. My hips were stiff. I didn't understand the teacher's cues. I was all up in my head and meditation wasn't in my vocabulary and certainly not going on between my ears. But I kept going. Three times a week. Back again and again.

And then it happened. There was a very special moment, probably about two months in, when something shifted. It felt more comfortable. Familiar. Safer, somehow. Just a little at first, and a lot more as time passed. Now, there's no place like the yoga mat for me, and, in time, you'll feel that too.

How much asana practice is enough? That has to do with many things: Where you are in your life. Where you are in your health. What it is you seek to gain. If there are certain objectives you wish to fulfill in terms of your health and well-being, then the amount of asana practice that's right for you is relative to those things.

So, here is how you can move into this first touchstone.

First, get on the mat. If you do, there are certain things that you will experience—it may take a little while, but it will come. You will experience more peace, freedom, happiness, kindness, compassion, self-awareness, thoughtfulness, flexibility, strength, a younger-looking body and skin, better digestion, more energy. If you don't go to the mat, you might be tired. You might not. You might feel weak. You might not. You might have energy. You might not. But we know that people who do yoga report feeling stronger, taller, more energized, more peaceful, more connected to their loved ones, and happier. Chances are, these things will also happen for you.

So if you've ever said, "I really need to do some yoga," I say, "Take a deep breath, hold space for the whiner in you, and then get on the mat." After all, we don't come to the mat to become anything. We come to the mat to be, to breathe. That is the practice.

The second piece to this touchstone is getting outside and doing something, anything, that allows for long and deep breathing: hiking, mucking stalls, walking, bicycling, bushwhacking to a waterfall, playing dog with the dogs (versus being a human watching the dogs play), or taking a few laps around a lake. Something where you are doused in nature and fresh clean air (think green spaces and parks versus streets and urban areas with high concentrations of people, buildings, and vehicles). Once again, that fresh air is super important when it comes to nourishing the body with movement. Being outdoors is king when it comes to awakening one's heart and happiness. And, if the lack of structure concerns you, you can add some sort of plan, such as time or distance. The point is to have the process not the outcome, the intention not the goal, be the point of focus and your measure for "success." "Did I get outside and do something?" becomes the question; then there is no puffing up or constricting as a result of how much you did or how fast you did it. Instead, you acknowledge that you did it. You got outside. You walked. You breathed. You used your big muscles. And you felt it—which, time will show you, is what makes the greatest difference. It's not a thinking thing. It's a feeling thing. And then, simply, it's a doing thing. And then... it is done.

Let's take a view from 10,000 feet, shall we?

The title of this book is Pilgrim: Living Your Yoga Every Single Day. In this way, I offer that moving your body is not about exercising. It's not about cardiovascular fitness. It's not about being able to do 24 yogi-style push-ups. It's not about any of those pieces; it's about recognizing that we start with this body. This is the very first touchstone because the human body is your material manifestation of all of your choices. This body is a living, breathing culmination of your life to date.

This physical body is what we call the anamaya kosha (modified food body) in Yoga. This is the most gross and the most tangible aspect of all that you are. Like your DNA reveals your ancestry, your body reveals your life experiences and your choices—conscious and unconscious. It reveals how you have devoted your time, your energy, your resources, your life force.

Think of your body as a vehicle, a really fancy ride, perhaps even your dream car. Just as movement is key for this vehicle, so too is stillness and meditation. If we don't sit and have moments of steadiness and recalibration, it's like driving your dream car and suddenly realizing that the brakes don't work. So if the brakes don't work and full speed ahead is your only option (ever feel that way in life?), your dream car can become a nightmare in a moment's notice. This is why we connect to both movement and stillness. In the traditional asana practices, which are very different from Western practices, one would go into asana for a while —do some postures, move, shift, work some things out in the body—and then come to stillness, come to rest. Then maybe do it again. Move, move, move, and then come to stillness. Movement and stillness must both be present and practiced to live in balance, in Yoga.

There is a way that we come to these practices, whether we speak of the mat practices or the getting outside, where we get beyond the physical and we focus on the breath—not because the breath delivers oxygen consumption and releases carbon dioxide, but because our breath carries our life force. And this life force, this prana, is always wanting to move with you, through you, in you. You are forming a relationship with it, moving, breathing, and responding to life.

Yoga will give you a thousandfold what you give it. This I know. The physical body is the vehicle. The physical body is the container. So we move, shift, care for, and honor this remarkable chariot through the continuum of movements and practices.

To review, this first touchstone has two basic components:
* Get on the mat (stream a practice online, go to a class, buy a DVD)
* Get outside

That's all. Go on now. Get.

One Simple Practice:
Choose one practice—either getting to the mat or getting outside—and do it before 9 am every single day for 13 days straight. If you miss the "before 9" window, let it shift to a 1 pm personal deadline. Stick with it. No back talk. No exceptions.

Touchstone #2: Purify My Vessel

You are a sacred vessel.

There's a line by the poet Rumi that says, "I am a hole in the flute through which the Divine's breath flows." When I first read this, I thought, "I'm just the hole? What the heck? I am not the flute... not the sweet music either... but just. the. hole!" Humbling, wouldn't you agree? And also incredibly liberating. For if I am the hole, all I have to do is keep what is not supposed to be in there outta there.

Each of us is merely and profoundly the hole, the space through which energy moves. And in this way, your body is the vessel. Your body is a channel, a conduit, and a physical manifestation designed to draw divine energy from around you through you, so it's important to keep your vessel free from blockages and debris.

Let's look at it this way: You are in a modified food body (the anamaya kosha, remember?) that is made up of broccoli and slices of bread and glasses of water and tea and tofu and whatever you might have been eating or drinking over these last few days. It might be all organic and pure and clean, and that's gorgeous, or it might be closer to the standard American diet—I'm not here to judge, and I offer that if you are feeling "judgey" toward yourself, you can let that go. As one of my early teachers said, "It's not the chocolate cake that will kill you; it's what you do to yourself over eating the chocolate cake that will kill you." In any case, we speak about the anamaya kosha as a physical manifestation of what we have taken into it over time. Your body is not who you are nor what you are. It is a vessel that you are using while you are here—nothing more, nothing less.

In this touchstone, we will focus on purifying the physical body as well as the more subtle aspects of who we are.

Here's an overview:
Body:
food, water, body care products, clothing
Mind:
music, thoughts, conversations, readings

Heart:
relationships, wounds, transgressions

Body:
Although the Purify My Vessel Refrigerator Chart and Seasonal
Produce Guide (link provided at the end of this book) are far
from exhaustive, they will give you a plenty big playground to begin to explore how you can purify the vessel of the physical body.
Some of the most obvious ways are by choosing high-quality,
well-sourced seasonal foods; pure, natural water; organic, non-
toxic body, skin, and hair care products; and clothing made of
fabrics that are natural and allow your body's largest organ (your
skin) to breathe.

The way I see it, a common-sense approach to revealing the brilliance that you are and keeping your body vessel pure and ready
for your highest intentions is your most important body-centered
objective in this life. It's simple: Your body is intended for pure
goodness.

Michael Pollan says, "Eat food. Mostly plants. Not too much."
This means eat that which is loaded with nutritional value and is
as close to its natural source as possible. Although I am not a
strict vegetarian and compassionately refer to myself as a "flexi-
tarian," I do my best to know the source and potency of all my
food, and to eat with the intention of paying forward whatever I
take into my body. Still, I'm not here to judge. I'm not here to say
you should or should not eat meat. I can tell you that the traditional Yogic perspective is to not eat meat, for doing so goes
against a profound and powerful universal law which states, "I
don't want to be hurt. You don't want to be hurt. No one wants to
be hurt."

This is an important matter. The fact is, taking yoga beyond a
mat practice includes a continuum of choices, and encourages
natural, non-harming choices whenever possible. This way, you
can be aligned with goodness and light through all you do. So if
you are eating meat, know your source. In this day and age, it's
quite easy to determine if there's a farmer in your area who sees

27

life as sacred the way you do. Meet local farmers, look them in the eyes, and dare to ask the hard questions. Recognize that an animal taken for food is not giving its life freely. When one eats animal, a divinely gifted life is being consumed. My hope is that we take this issue to heart. If you are an animal eater, you can keep these things in mind, and when you eat that animal, soften your heart and awaken reverence. Let it be a place where you take that in and recognize the sacredness of life and then make a commitment to pay forward that life force in goodness on the planet.

After all, everything is energy. What you take into your body is energy. It's physical energy, emotional and mental energy, it's spiritual and sacred energy. In recognizing that, your life as you move forward becomes graced with what it is you seek if you choose to infuse your life in these moments with goodness.

Further, moderation is key no matter what we eat. Moderate consumption is very important in the big picture—I reckon it is much more important than we give it credit for being. Eating too much food renders the body preoccupied with digestion and assimilation. The ancient Yogis tell you to fill your tummies 1/2 with food and 1/4 with liquid, and leave 1/4 of the stomach empty. You can see the value of such a formula in a blender, for example, and this same formula works in your own body so that what comes in is sufficiently combined, assimilated, and utilized without excess life force being dedicated to managing the surplus. When you eat an adequate but not excessive amount, your digestion works better and you rise in the morning rested and ready for the day.

Regarding your Purify My Vessel refrigerator chart, If you keep your home well stocked with the items in the "Fill" column, and reach for these first and foremost, the end result is a clean diet and a lot of spare vitality to use for things other than digestion. Letting go of items in the "Empty" column is the other approach. Further, if you follow the Seasonal Produce guide, you begin to align yourself with nature, filling your body naturally with the good stuff, and the result is there simply isn't much room left for the not-so-good stuff.

We've talked about what we do eat. Now let's talk about what/ when not to eat. One of my favorite approaches is to honor a 12-hour period (generally 7 pm–7 am) where I do not consume anything but clear decaffeinated liquids. I call it a 12-hour purifying practice. If you'd like, you can try this too. Purifying for 12 hours will give your body an opportunity to rest and to assimilate any of the "leftovers" in your body. It is amazing how honoring this 12-hour purify practice translates into more energy. You will find yourself feeling rested with less sleep, will have a more restful sleep, and will awaken with fewer aches and pains and more energy for the day.

Now let's go beyond the digestive system and talk about what you put on your body. Through the lens of Yoga, if you can put something on your body, you should be able to put it in your body. In other words, your body care products ought to be, technically, edible. Your skin is a large and luxurious organ that digests in its own way, and what you put on your body affects your health.

Here are a few ways you can begin to make some subtle changes: Look to your medicine cabinet and/or bathroom cupboard. Identify which items that are not edible are almost gone and start researching replacements so you don't impulsively buy the same product. Do a simple search online for healthy versions of [insert general product category]. My favorite brands are Alba, Dr. Hauschka, Shikai, Nature's Gate, and Weleda, but there are many others. You will be surprised at how far make-up, hair and body care products, soaps, and toothpastes have come. See which of these would be the easiest step to take in making a subtle but meaningful upgrade to the purification of your vessel.

You also put clothing on your body. We don't often think about clothing in terms of affecting our health, but the more we can move toward natural fibers as a rule, the less toxic our clothing will be. Personally, I love linen, cashmere, wool, and cotton, and with a little sleuthing at second-hand stores, vintage shops, eBay, and even contemporary stores, I am a walking testimonial that it

29

is relatively easy to begin replacing items in your closets and bureau with healthier options without breaking the bank.

Mind:
The vessel is more than the physical body. It is also the mind. To keep this simple, you can turn your attention to the quality of music, conversation, thoughts, and written material you interact with. Together, these things represent a fairly good cross-section of what we bring into our manamaya kosha (mental/emotional body). The first of these is music: Imagine if a particular song was a mirror for your life; would your life look as you desire? If not, you can choose something different to fill your ears, focusing on positive lyrics, heartfelt musicians, and only that which reflects how and who you want to be. My favorites are Michael Franti, MaMuse, Tina Malia, Shimshai, Girish, and Trevor Hall. (You can get a list of my favorite music at brittbsteele.com/Pilgrim-Jewels. Tether every sound back to a meaningful intention. Your ears are your highest sense organ, connecting you to the subtle, from which all things come and to which all things return. The little things really matter. And they become "matter"—which ultimately becomes your life.

Similarly, thoughts and conversations, with yourself and others, fit here too. Be conscious about what you say to yourself and to others, for "thoughts become things" and everything moves from the subtle to manifest. It is described beautifully in Sanskrit: Yat Bhavam Tad Bhavati. This is one of my favorite prayerful reminders, and translates in English to: "As you worship, so you become."

Worship? Yes, worship. Worship is your devotion. To what do you devote your time? Your energy? Your breath? What you talk about—to yourself and others—is what you become... So complaining, honoring the mundane—the material, the unconscious, the meaningless (hair, nails, shoes, cars, vacations, etc.)—matters. And remember, it isn't as simple as what you talk about; it has even more to do with what aspects of your conversation you are devoting yourself to: Beauty? Heart connections? Love? Yes.

Fashion? The world's biggest Ferris wheel? Life-size cartoon characters? That convertible you rented? Not so much.

And finally, there is what you are reading: books, magazines, on-line subscriptions, blogs—same same. Here's the simplest way I can describe it: If you imagine you're 108 years old, looking back at your bookshelf, your coffee table, the websites you book-marked, your closet, your pantry, your cabinets—kitchen and medicine—would what you see create a path of consciousness to your life at 108? And in reverse, would what you are choosing now pave a conscious pathway to what you want to be, think, feel, and do at 108 years old? Think about this, because what you are doing now is paving a pathway to your future. It is and it will con-tinue to do so. Be careful what you choose, for if you do not choose consciously, you are choosing unconsciously. Your future is being manifest with every microcosmic choice you make in your every now. Now. Now.

Heart:
On a slightly more manifest level are the relationships you cur-rently have, how they are impacting your heart, and how you might be able to purify your heart. I will confess that this section will not do justice to the wisdom that Yoga has to share on this topic, but there are some key considerations:

> **You are the source of your own happiness.**
> **You are the source of your own suffering.**
> **All of it.**
> **Once you get this, you get everything.**

Whew. What? Yep. That's something you can meditate on for about 108 days all on its own, and your heart would bloom wide and brilliantly.

And here's the other thing with this: Whatever challenges you ex-perience in your relationships, I offer up that the #1 way to make a huge difference in how you feel about those challenges, that re-lationship, and that person is to offer it to the altar. Give it all back to the Ultimate Giver, the one who has given you every blessing, every challenge, every opportunity, and every breath. There is only one Giver—and that Giver will take it all back with glad acceptance. Taking your challenges, your struggle, your perceptions willingly and with full receptivity. Bringing your diatribe, your complaints, your transgressions and wounds to another person at some point along the way will not be nearly as effective as bringing it all back and placing it in the lap of the divine. Just like a mama holds space for a toddler in a tantrum, with love and compassion, and dispassion, so too does the divine universe/mother/father/call it what works for you hold us in our struggles.

Old relationship wounds, mistakes, affairs, losses, and screw-ups —your own and others'—lay them down too. Write that letter and burn it. Pray for release. Give up making it right with that person, unless your lack of forgiveness is holding them somehow—then forgive. But if you are the one you are holding hostage in non-forgiveness, then to the altar you go. More about this in a later touchstone. But for now, lay it down. It's not yours. What you did is not who you are. Never was. Never will be. Lay. It. Down.

Here's the deal: If all you did for these 108 days was to go, first thing in the morning, to your "special place" and sit in conscious, divine prayer with the good ol' Serenity Prayer, your world would change—in a good way.

Here it is, my favorite, written as a Yogi might take it:

Oh Lord, infinite intelligent being,
who is not separate from myself,
please bestow upon me the inner peace and serenity
to accept gracefully all that I cannot change...
Like the past, other people, anything that has
been said or done to me.
And may I have the strength and courage
to change what I can change—in my life, now.
What is within my power to do so...
such as certain habits, or what I say in each moment,
my words... and what I do.

And may I understand and see clearly.
May I have the wisdom to recognize what I am able to
change, and what I am not able to change,
so that I do not waste my will...
so that I do not waste my energy... nor the energy
of another... trying to change what I cannot.
So that I am a manifestation of goodness,
clear vision, and pure light.
Om Shanthi. Shanthi. Shanthi.

One Simple Practice:
Print your Purify My Vessel and Seasonal Produce Guide Refrigerator Charts and highlight five items you intend to bring into your body every single day. Underline one item you will eliminate—slowly, if need be—over the course of a 13-day period.

Touchstone #3: Join Conscious Community

What is Conscious Community?

Simply put, this touchstone is about the realization that the people with whom you spend your time either support your highest unfolding or... well... they don't. This doesn't mean you don't hang with them, or that you harshly excommunicate your family from your life. It means that if they aren't raising you up, and you want to end up somewhere light and bright, you need to bring the consciousness to the table... to the potluck... to the family reunion or the company party.

Every day, every breath, every moment, you can seek out people who live lives that you adore and make manifest the qualities you revere in your own life.

Joining Conscious Community is another thing... It's about "joining." It is about coming together, as human beings, in a way that is awake and alert. Seeing and holding space for one another, without intending to change one another, nor having an agenda of any sort. Instead, you're focusing your personal intention on being awake, true to your ideals and aspirations, while being in the presence of others who are also wanting to be conscious, reveal their best self, see, be seen, hold space, and release their agendas for themselves, others, the world, and God.

Whew! Let's look at that again: Conscious community is focusing one's personal intention on being awake, true to your ideals and aspirations, while being in the presence of others who are also wanting to be conscious, reveal their best self, see, be seen, hold space, and release their agendas for themselves, others, the world, and God.

That is a hefty order, no doubt. But through aligning your personal intentions within and without, you will find that you can create conscious community in your life, and reap the huge bounty of living in sacred connection and purpose.

Connection is integral to community. Humans are a species of connectivity. Humans are communal beings, tribal and interconnected. You know the power of being supported, being seen, and

36

being socially integrated with those who see the best in you and hold you to loving, honest standards. There is immense value in having your emotions and experiences validated, and when you experience this, you are gifted with seeing a reflection of your true self as being important, worthy, and whole. And when you see yourself in this way, you see others through this same lens. And everybody gets just a little bit of happy.

HAPPY
is the foundation of consciousness.
CONSCIOUSNESS
is the foundation for being happy.

What, exactly, is "happy"?

For our purposes, there are two kinds of happy, neither of which necessitates being the life of the party, the charismatic outgoing sort, or even always wearing a smile, saying nice things, or being the star helper when someone is in need. Through the lens of Yoga, "happy" is way bigger than that. Happy is your true nature.

There's the first kind of happy:

The first kind of happy I will call "relative happiness," meaning the kind of happiness you feel "relative" to what is going on in your life. This is where you experience a state—a state of "happiness" in relation to the weather, the economy, your health, the lives of those you love, and the things that are most important to you. The tricky part about this first kind of happy is that it is affected by what is going on around you. When good things are happening around you, you feel happy. When things around you go sour, happiness wanes. This is the way of relative happiness.

Then, there's the second kind of happy: the kind that lasts.

So, you've got your relative happiness that is affected by whether you have enough food in your tummy, your loved ones are safe, your body is functioning properly, you've got a job you like, the sun is shining. You know, the whole spectrum of things that affect us, from the big things to the little things.

But then... then you've got the second kind of happy. We'll call this "absolute happiness." This is, as it is described, absolute. Absolute means that it is free from any outside influence or affect, that it is full and complete as part of its nature, in and through all transient conditions of weather, wealth, health, or status. Absolute means full and having everything that is needed as part and parcel of itself. So, in this way, absolute happiness is the real deal. It's there when you are strong and fit, thin and gorgeous, and it is there when you are sick, tired, in deep sleep, old, and even when you are no longer here—aka "dead." This kind of happy, through the lens of Yoga, is related to the anandamaya kosha—the most subtle layer of oneself that is fully and completely blissed out, also known as happy.

Through the wise and ancient Yogic lens, you don't need anything at all from the outside to make you happy. You are happiness in and through all external circumstances—whatever they may be. You prevail. Therefore, happiness prevails. And that, dear friends, is why I call this "the real deal" kind of happy.

Now, just because someone (me) tells someone else (you) that "you are happiness itself," it isn't as though a magic wand is waved over your head and POOF! You're happy. We both know that is not how these things work.

Ultimately, that's where the consciousness comes in. It has to start with you. You are the first place from which happiness happens, and in the beginning, you've gotta practice, practice, practice resetting to "happy"—no matter what or who says otherwise. Happiness is a choice. In the beginning, it feels more like a chore. But in time, there are subtle shifts that occur, and happiness comes easier and easier, moving farther from that point of needing something to "make" you happy and more toward happiness being the "default" to which you return when there isn't something challenging you. In this way, you are able to access and realize happiness as a "trait" instead of a "state" influenced by what is going on around you.

So, you practice. And again and again you choose to return to happy—as your default. It takes some focus at first, for you may have a tendency, a survival impulse, to look for and look out for what might cause you trouble, as a means to keep yourself from harm. Once you realize this survival mechanism, you can let go of that impulse to focus on what's not working, and only revert to that propensity in life when absolutely necessary.

I am not suggesting that you shrug your shoulders at the clouds, fake it 'til you make it, or default to plastering a smile on your face, playing Pollyanna. Quite the contrary, actually. I am suggesting that you enter each moment of your life with eyes wide open and heart softened... receiving everything... taking it all in and noticing where you feel charged and then returning, again and again, to the reality that you are not the world, its choices, its manifestation. Nor are you your choices. In this way, you will slowly steer the large ship of your life toward happy, and the things on the outside will be seen, acknowledged, and accepted as they are, and then you can get in there and change what you can (remember the Serenity Prayer?).

The take-home message is to see things as they are. Keep what is outside of you outside of you... and return again and again to your breath, to eyes open, and heart softened, and there... here is where you will be ready to meet on equal footing the conscious community you crave.

Like I said before, "consciousness is the foundation for happiness, and happiness is the foundation for consciousness." So, we've talked about consciousness by way of happiness. Now let's talk community. Conscious community.

Conscious community begins with your own consciousness reaching out to other pilgrims, seekers, and teachers who have found their way, and making it known through your presence and honest expression that connecting with them is sacred to you.

In the beginning, creating conscious community can feel like choosing a whole bunch of cooler people than you perceive yourself to be to spend your time with so that, if you're lucky, they will rub off on you. This is partly true. Because, ultimately, what they are doing is not just "rubbing off on you" but they are rubbing up against you (being your touchstone) so your brilliance can be revealed. The reason you feel good around those amazing people is because they offer you back to yourself in a way that is human and visible. They serve as your reminder and your mirror. So, joining conscious community is manifesting a circle of support, reflection, and inspiration, and aligning hearts all around you so that when you set an intention for yourself to be in your own fullness and brilliance, the embodiment of that becomes easy. All arrows point to yes, point to seeing yourself as absolute happiness in and through. Then your life becomes a magical manifestation of a litany of little things that make you know yourself as full and complete without the world, others, yourself, or God needing to be different, not even a little. Everything is whole. Just as it is. And who doesn't want to feel that?

So, now, let's talk about how you get to this. In my experience, it's about admiration. For as you admire, so you worship, and you've already learned Yad Bhavam Tad Bhavati, that as you worship, so you become. Admiration stems from a desire to know, a wondering with high intention. And the qualities you admire in others, the qualities you wonder about and wonder how you might bring into your being, are where this all begins. These qualities are energetic attributes that you see, that inspire you, and that open you. You "see" with your eyes, but it isn't like seeing a stop sign, because there is magnetism. There is a heartfelt calling to which you are drawn, as if your whole body is saying, "I want some of that!" You see and experience others through a lens of respect and worth. You see and experience a life being led in alignment, and through this alignment, this other person or persons become the pathway you, yourself, walk toward God. (Now, don't get hung up on that word—for it is three little letters that can never be as limited as thought, nor as powerful as the entire manifest universe and the One who made it manifest). Anyway, it's a sweet, sweet setup.

Here is a list of qualities you might admire. You can use this list and add other qualities to make it your own:

SELF-DISCIPLINED	PATIENT
BEAUTY	INTELLIGENCE
HONESTY	HUMILITY
TRANSPARENCY	HUMOR
APPROACHABLE	HEALTHY
LIGHT-HEARTEDNESS	RESPONSIVE
TRUSTWORTHY	RELIABLE
VISIONARY	FREE
COMPASSIONATE	TENACIOUS
SERVICE-ORIENTED	MYSTICAL
ORGANIZED	LOVING
INTEGRATED	THOUGHTFUL
SPIRITUAL	STEADFAST
GENTLE	SIMPLE
MODEST	GENEROUS
PEACEFUL	RADIANT
EXUBERANT	ARTICULATE
COMMUNICATIVE	CONFIDENT
FEARLESS	CREATIVE
STRAIGHTFORWARD	BALANCED
PURE-HEARTED	APPRECIATIVE

Then, use the following exercise to help you tease out what works for you in creating conscious community.

#1. Take a look at the list and quickly circle the qualities you admire most. There is no need at this point to have anyone in particular in mind, no need to value one quality over another (e.g., patience is "better" than beauty). Just trust and circle what you admire most.

#2. Take the list of your circled qualities and write them in your journal. Sit with them for a few moments and see if they are truly qualities you admire. You might ask yourself, When someone is [insert quality here], how do I feel? Then, you can ask yourself,

Do I want to feel that way? Why? And what is the benefit/how will my life be different if I feel that way? This is a useful cross-check you can use to go a little deeper. Then, if any qualities need to be removed or edited, or if you feel like you are missing something, add, delete, or modify as you see fit.

#3. Next, look out into your life at your close-knit community, the places you socialize, your neighbors, your interactions (in places like the local library, the stores where you buy groceries or household supplies, your favorite restaurant, or a recent party or meeting you attended). Write down a few names of people you would love to get to know better, spend time with, or consciously connect with. It is important to note that it doesn't matter if you know these people well at this stage. They are simply people that emulate the qualities you admire, and so you are bringing your attention to these people, and, most importantly, the qualities manifest within.

#4. Here's the vulnerable, powerful part. Choose two people, possibly the ones that feel the most accessible to you at this point, decide how you would like to connect with them, and reach out. If you know them really well, or if you don't know them well at all, doing this step will likely elicit feelings of vulnerability, but how well you know someone isn't the point. The point is that you are recognizing something you admire, choosing a person that represents these qualities to you, and reaching out to them. You could send a note or a card, call them, bring them a flower or a jar of your favorite homemade balm or jam…Just something, anything "thoughtful" (don't judge what is thoughtful, just think about it—with your heart, perhaps—and then share accordingly). And then you say something—in person, in writing, or on the phone—something like this…

Dear [insert name]—

It was great to meet you at [insert how you met]. That [meeting, get-together, etc.] was so nice, and for me, it was extra special to connect with people of like mind. I

am on a personal mission to cultivate meaningful connections with people of like mind and heart, and you seem to fit that description. I admire [include quality you admire and any other details here, such as: how light-hearted you are and how the room lights up and how comfortable people seem to be when you come in]. I would love to connect for lunch or tea if you've the time—[add ways they can contact you here].
In any case, just wanted you to know that I see you and see how magnificent of a human being you are.

♥,
[You]

Notice how the touchstone reads "Join Conscious Community." That is you, babe. Joining up your consciousness with collective consciousness. You don't have to create it. It's not that kind of work. You are here, and community is here, and all you need to do is breathe, set your intention, take some baby steps, do your best each day with what you are given, and then watch the beauty unfold. Community happens when there is more than one person. Wherever two or more are gathered? With meaningful, sacred intention? You just joined yourself up in some conscious community!

One Simple Practice:
Make a phone call today—just one—to someone you know will raise you up. If you don't get them personally (and find yourself leaving a message), plant the seed to get a call-back and then choose someone else until you get someone on the phone. Express your admiration and desire to connect with people who inspire you.

Touchstone #4: Find Sacred Space

Your home is where you hit "sacred reset".

Sacred space is everything that surrounds your essential nature—from the microcosm to the macrocosm. From the sheets you put on your bed, to the lotion you put on your face at night, to the connections to which you tend in your neighborhood or your community. Your "space" is sacred. And when you realize this and make manifest a reverence for all things, you become relaxed and selective with how you move through life and formulate even the slightest decisions.

For this touchstone, I will jump right in with an exercise. If you choose to just read about this versus doing it now, promise yourself that you will come back and do it later. It is very powerful. Either way, read it first, without projecting or jumping ahead. Just take in the instructions, resisting the urge to catapult yourself forward into mentally doing it before you actually do it in person.

Here it is: Go outside, and then enter your home as if you have never seen it before, as if it is the first time ever walking through your door. Walk in, notice your initial impression, and then take a seat. Practice being a "witness" and look around—without judgment. Notice what you see. Look at what you have collected, purchased, brought into your space, and notice what it says—where's it from? From what materials are your furniture and fixtures made? What benefits or loss resulted from your purchase or acceptance of this into your home—for you or for another? How do you feel when you see these things? What did you bring in consciously? What did you bring in unconsciously? Pay attention, and then go to your journal and write three things that you learned.

Next, look more closely at what you call your home. Bring your attention to your personal home—your body, your skin, your clothes, the shape and state of your being—and do the same practice, noticing where it has come from and from what it is made. Your weight, your form, your hair (natural or colored?), your adornments (jewelry, polishes, clothing). You can call it "woo woo" if you choose, but hear me when I say that when you look around your home, your space, and even your body, what you see is exactly as it is as a result of the culmination of your choices—both conscious and unconscious. This is exciting! (I say that particularly to those who just contracted in reaction to being responsible for what they see.) Truly, it is exciting to come to this realization, for just as you have created your life "as is," so too can you create something else, and something so much more.

If you are anything like me (which of course you are, because we are all the same at the root of this stuff), you found that there are some things that you have chosen to bring into your space that feel very sacred, while there are other things that feel meaningless or maybe even completely opposite what you claim as important to you and aligned with your current intentions.

In this touchstone we will cover a few basic categories, but before we do, I'll also offer that you can extrapolate any of these observances and consciousness practices to any "space" in your life, close and far (think your nightstand or the space you occupy throughout your day-to-day life).

Okay, let's find sacred space. For each area of your home discussed below, I include general tips for creating sacred space and then provide more specifics for the most important aspects.

Bedroom:
Sacred space, indeed! This may be the place in the house where you are the most vulnerable, where you seek to recalibrate more fully than any other space. It is where you slip into sleep and deep sleep and receive nature's imprint.

Ways to find sacred space in the bedroom:
- Bedding made from natural fibers
- Non-toxic ambiance (candles, scents, etc.)
- Bathe before bedtime
- Technology fast before sleep
- Minimize electro-magnetic frequencies
- Sleep with the window cracked open

- Awaken naturally or to a gentle alarm
- Time without technology upon waking

Bedding: This one is simple; the key word for bedding is natural. Choose linen, cotton, cotton flannel, Tencel, hemp, or wool. No synthetic blends, no polyester, no "minky," no polar fleece, no soft fuzzy fabrics—these feel great to the touch but are often made of petroleum products. Here's the thing—you are made of natural materials. You want the rest you get to be as sound and recalibrating as possible. "Dis-ease" arises when we are out of alignment, and this can happen when our internal environment is getting mixed messages from our external environment. And remember, baby steps; you don't necessarily have to throw everything out and start over.

Ambiance: As far as the rest of your bedroom goes, choose candles, incense, scents, etc. that are natural and close to their original source in nature. Be cognizant of your alarm clock—in a perfect world, choose a battery-operated one (or forego one altogether if you have that luxury). Avoid having your phone sitting by your head, and if it must be on your nightstand, put it on airplane mode to give your body a break from all of the toxicity and strong electro-magnetic frequencies (EMFs) that bombard us daily. The truth is, we don't know for sure the spectrum of impact that EMFs, toxic ingredients, and synthetic fabrics have on the body. But we do know that when we live in community with nature, we rest more deeply, awaken more refreshed, and suffer less from the litany of "diseases of affluence" (heart disease, auto-immune conditions, some cancers, anxiety, depression, and nervous system disorders, to name a few).

Some of my favorite brands: The Honest Co., Pacifica, and Mrs. Meyers

Bathroom:
This space is where you anoint your body and absorb the content and impact of whatever is applied.

Ways to find sacred space in the bathroom:
- All-natural cleaning supplies
- Cotton towels and robes
- Good air flow (window + fan)
- Non-toxic ambiance (candles, scents, etc.)
- Natural, organic skin and hair care products

Cleaning Products: There's a theme you'll hear again and again and it applies here too: Go natural. Eliminate (or significantly decrease the use of) toxic cleaners, bleach, synthetic ingredients, and antibacterials. I search Vitacost.com for "organic" or "natural" cleaning supplies and find their pricing to be very competitive. (They also do a lovely job of packaging with recycled materials.) Some of my favorite brands: Ecover, Seventh Generation, BioKleen, and EarthFriendly

Personal Products: Pay attention to the products that are closest to your skin and hair, especially lotions, shampoos, and toothpastes. The point in creating sacred space is to ensure that you are doing what you can to return to what is natural, in its intended state (how it showed up here on the earth), and therefore give your body the best opportunity to know how to utilize it and/or dispose of it.

Some of my favorite brands: Weleda, Alba, Shikai, Dr. Hauschka, and Nature's Gate (again, Vitacost.com is one of my go-to sources to purchase these items)

For both cleaning and personal products, I encourage you to explore DIY options as well. Through the lens of Ayurveda, the holistic medical side of Yoga, every product that is used on the skin, hair, and body ought to be non-toxic if consumed—which makes sense because your skin, hair, and entire body are "consuming" these products. Search on Pinterest or Google to find recipes for DIY body care products and cleaning supplies and give them a try.

Office:
Whatever kind of work you do, and wherever you do it, your office or workspace is incredibly sacred, for it is where you move your life force through and share it with the world.

Ways to find sacred space in the office:
- Items that reflect your values and intentions
- Adequate, natural air flow
- Proper lighting
- Healthy ergonomics
- A timer to remind you to take breaks

Oh, the office (sigh)... this space is incredibly personal, because it is where you are consciously aligning your internal intentions with the world. It doesn't matter if you cut hair or are a book-keeper, artist, writer, or yoga teacher—be clear on the space that you consider to be your primary workspace and shift your perspective on what makes this space sacred to you. Further, if you don't have a specific space, I recommend you identify one. There is something powerful about establishing space as part of your ritual for prayer, nourishment, self-care, and creation. Having a space where you always always go programs subtle neurological circuitry that allows you to access clarity, trust, and ease.

It's powerful to be reminded about who you are, what you do, and why you do it. It is important to be clear on the vision of your work in the world, the need you fill, and the one thing that you can offer the world that the world would benefit the most from. Post these reminders throughout your space.

Your gifts are to be shared with the world, and there is nothing that is not sacred. You can see tax preparation, inventory management, quality control, truck driving, team management, or package labeling as sacred. You just gotta put your sacred glasses on!

What does that mean? Ask yourself these questions:
- How does what I do make others' lives better?
- How is what I am doing making the world a better place?

- What is it about my space that I see as sacred?
- How can I see what I do as divine service?
- What ritual or practice can I do daily to create a meaning-ful (call it prayerful if you'd like) environment for myself and those with whom I interact?
- How can I do what I do in a way that honors me and the work I do in a more devotional way?

There are little things that you can do in your work day, and in your work space (whether you work at home or not), to bring forth a sense that the way you touch others is in kindness, truth, and love. That is all there is, after all.

Kitchen:
Here is where you nourish. Where your life force meets up with universal life force. This is where the vibration of life around you affects the vibration of life within you and those you nourish.

Ways to find sacred space in the kitchen:
- Fresh spices, condiments, and jarred products
- Sacred offering space (nearest the NE corner)
- Natural cookware: cast iron, steel, glass, clay, stoneware
- Minimally processed ingredients
- Non-toxic storage containers
- Fresh and organic produce
- Limited animal products
- Everything in exquisite moderation

This section could be an entire book in and of itself, and I'm not going to go into too much detail here, but remember that even little things make a huge difference. Look at small, meaningful, sustainable steps you can take: Clean out your refrigerator, empty your cabinets of any canned or non-perishable goods older than one year. Donate acceptable items to your local food bank. Dispose of any old water bottles and food storage containers that have lost their integrity or contain BPA, and consider removing or at least not using any non-stick pots and pans, aluminum pans, and your microwave. (I know this sounds huge, but I promise you'll get used to it and grow to love this hub of nourishment even more! You'll never miss any of it. I swear!)

It is also really wonderful to have a quiet space in your kitchen where you have a candle and maybe a single stem flower in a vase. I do this in the NE corner; this is the ether element corner, which is where we are reminded that all food comes from God (Nature, Goddess, Brahma, the One, you name him/her, whomever-she-he-may-be-to-you)... and you consciously, soulfully, gratefully prepare your food for your self and others. This is your little "altar" in your kitchen where you count your blessings and offer back every bit of life force that you have been given to the ultimate and only Giver. (After all, think about it... isn't there only ultimately one Giver?)

Offer everything back to the Ultimate Giver
There is only one Giver
You are not the Doer
You are the one through whom
all doing flows
You are the conduit for sacred life force
No matter what you do,
you can do so with reverence and with holy, sacred nourishment

So we've covered the primary locations where you can find sacred space in your home and in your life. You can extrapolate these practices and sacred observances to your studio, your vehicle, your living room, your yoga space, your office. The point in all of it is that "sacred" is the lens through which you see what is. It isn't about your house, your space, or your world being perfect. It is about recognizing that everything is whole and that we do the best with what we have and when we have not done our best, we just do a little bit to make it better. Then, we let go. The only difference between the sacred world and the material world is the lens through which you see what is before your very eyes.

Sacred rituals for anytime and any place.:

- Fill your ears with music that is healthy and nourishing- Subscribe to magazines and publications that "average you up (toward the light)" and inspire you to show your best self
- Read books that embody health, vitality, purpose, intention, and sacred connection
- Choose household "pretty things" that have been made through fair trade, will not be thrown in a landfill when you redecorate, and have meaning to you beyond "Oh! Isn't that pretty?"
- Consider bringing live, fresh flowers or sprigs into your home once a week, if only a branch from a tree in your backyard or a fern from beside the sidewalk

One Simple Practice:

Do a quick walk-through of your house: kitchen, bathroom, bedroom. Look around (open a drawer or cabinet if necessary) and identify 1–3 things that you'd like to replace or "upgrade" to reveal more sacredness in your space. Then upgrade or replace these things.

Touchstone #5: Align With Nature

Your nature *is* nature.

Other than the clothes you wear to suit the weather outside, you may seldom consider the elements as having an impact on your day-to-day choices. For example, it is less than common to consider the weather when selecting food, sleep patterns, and your yoga practice. You set your alarm, awake when it is time to get kids to school or go to work, and rarely consider resting with the cycle of the moon or taking into consideration how your digestion, adrenal function, or liver health is being influenced by what is happening outside.

The truth is that there is weather outside (of you) and weather inside (of you). The same elements that exist in and through all of nature and affect your natural surroundings also exist in and through every cell in your body and affect your internal landscape. This touchstone is about how you can bring certain considerations into your awareness and practice that will help balance your internal "nature" with the planet and life as a whole, resulting in a stronger connection to all that is, and provide an early indication and conscious pattern to shift when things begin to feel out of balance.

When you look outside and see trees budding, wind blowing, snow falling, or leaves changing, these are all physical manifestations of the relationship between the five elements: earth, water, fire, air, and ether. When it comes to personal health, potency, and the ability to journey through life's ups and downs, as well as to have the stamina, clarity, vision, and power to walk the pilgrim's path, understanding and integrating these five elements is integral to doing life in a way that feels really good and has some serious purpose.

In Yoga we call these five elements pancha maha bhuta, and they are considered to be the basis of all of creation. Through this lens there are, indeed, five elements, even though you cannot see ether (sometimes called space). Ether is incredibly important, despite its invisibility, and shares equal place as one of the pancha maha bhuta. In this way, all things come from space and return to space. It exists in and through everything, so therefore it must be included, for it is "elemental" to both our understanding and embodiment of life itself.

The words we use express the elements and the elements express our lives.

Prithvi (earth)
Jal (water)
Agni (fire)
Vayu (air)
Aakash (ether)

Earth element
Prithvi

Earth element is the most gross and obvious of the five elements. It is the element that you can touch, see, build up, and upon, and that which holds you each day as you walk this Earth. It exists in everything that has form and is essential to everything in the material world. All material possessions, including your very own body, are made of earth element. Phrases like "I'm stuck," "It matters," or "I'm firm on this" all represent the influence of Earth.

Earth in balance feels: grounded, stable, rooted, steady, and structural. Our bodies feel strong and capable, and we firmly and solidly inhabit this body and this life.

Earth out of balance feels: stuck, depressed, weighed down, and heavy. Getting out of bed, moving your body, and doing anything—even the fun stuff—feels like a burden.

Balancing practices for Earth:
- Take brisk, long walks in nature early in the day (6–10 am)
- Asana practice in the mornings is best (6–10 am), with a focus on active movement, entire body stimulation, raising one's body temperature, and meeting new challenges with zest!

- Connect with friends that make you laugh
- Watch funny movies and socialize regularly
- Listen to uplifting music
- Keep your windows open (even when it's cold—crack them)
- Eat seasonally and very fresh—avoid meat, fried and fatty foods, heavy sauces, excessive oil, and processed, canned, or frozen foods)
- Avoid alcohol
- Caffeinated drinks in the morning may be medicinal (for lethargy as an example)
- Write anonymous love letters
- Send anonymous care packages
- Volunteer your time and energy to something where there is a lot of energy, such as with children, nature, or animals

Water element
Jal

Water element is known in the west as the "universal solvent," and through the lens of Yoga it is responsible for attracting, bonding, and transporting nutrients. It manifests in your body as plasma, mucous, sexual juice, fluids, and blood. It is the river upon which life flows and allows us to be in connection with one another, in intimacy and nourishment.

Water in balance feels: fluid, juicy, and naturally able to navigate the twists and turns of life. Our skin is supple and our joints well lubricated. We can easily shape shift and take many forms, moving quickly when life offers rapid change, and feel comfortable in stillness and quietude.

Water out of balance feels: boundaryless and overwhelming. Life itself feels chaotic and torrid, leaving us with a feeling that we can't hold ourselves or our "stuff" together, and we are left feeling like we need someone or something to keep us from falling apart.

Balancing practices for Water:

- Create ritual that help you clarify your individual likes and dislikes
- Practice balanced breathing (equal inhale count to eight, equal exhale count to eight)—do this often
- Go for walks alone in the rain
- Practice strong asana practices with structure and stick with it (choose a 13-day stint and do it every single day—don't skimp, don't cheat—maybe it's a 40-minute practice; whatever structure you set up for yourself and stick with it)
- Take yourself on a date (yes, alone)
- Make love
- Give freely to others—expect nothing in return
- Eat moderately and seasonally, avoiding caffeine, poultry, fish, goat, alcohol, and eating after 7 pm
- Rise with the sun and go to bed with the sun

Fire element
Agni

Fire element is known for transformation and digestion. Within the body, it predominantly manifests as maintaining a comfortable body temperature, assimilation of nutrients, and igniting the spark of intelligence. Fire governs our will center and moves us upward (like a flame rises) toward our goals and intentions. We can see the power of fire through the radiance of the sun and the potency of a single candle flame.

Fire in balance feels: warm, clear, bright, and brilliant. New ideas come easily and others are drawn toward us for we ignite their vibrance and clarity just by being near them.

Fire out of balance feels: hot, sharp, and erratic. You feel unpredictable and sharp-tongued, and others tend to not want to be close to you to avoid being "burned."

Balancing practices for Fire:

- Go on meandering adventures, without goals
- Practice asana flows to open the heart
- Allow for much rest, meditation, and gentle breathing
- Practice balanced breathing (equal inhale count to eight, equal exhale count to eight) laced into the asana practice
- Avoid inversions if heat is raised in the body
- Drink water with lime, mint, or rosewater
- Eat seasonally and fresh
- Avoid spicy foods, meat, alcohol, and caffeine
- Get massage regularly
- Buy yourself flowers
- Hold babies and puppies whenever the opportunity presents itself
- Stay out of direct sunlight and practice moderate activity (mental, physical, and emotional) from 10 am to 2 pm

Air element
Vayu

Air element is known predominantly for the action of movement. Although the word vayu literally translates to "wind," this does not describe the power and potency of vayu. Within the body, it manifests as the electrical energy in the nervous system, movement of all tissues and cell functions, and the formation of gases. It governs all of the senses due to its affinity with the nervous system and specifically the sense of touch and the action of the hands to give and receive.

Air in balance feels: mobile and inspirational. Our mind perceives few limitations and we recognize that boundaries are not limitations, after all. We know the sky is the limit. We may see the unseeable, and realize there is much more than what appears to be real. This inspires us and inspires others.

Air out of balance feels: dry, agitated, and unable to clearly define most anything. We tend toward insomnia, nervousness, overactivity, talking too much, interrupting, and feeling ungrounded, nervous, and unstable.

Balancing practices for Air.

- Choose asana practices that are strong and steady, and require long deep breaths and strong muscular holds (think slow and steady)
- Get deep-tissue bodywork regularly
- Take baths
- Avoid internet, radio, television, conversation, or reading one hour before bed
- Eat seasonally and fresh—slow cooking is best
- Avoid cold drinks, cold foods, crispy dry foods (such as raw apples, crackers, chips, dried fruit, etc.)
- Avoid poultry, ice cream, and raw foods
- Lunar breathing: Inhale through the left nostril to the count of six, exhale through the right nostril to the count of six, and continue inhaling only through the left and exhaling only through the right to a count of six for 10 rounds

Ether element
Aakash

Ether (sometimes called space) is the most subtle and pervasive of all five elements. It exists in all other elements and therefore in all things. Because of this, it is whole and complete, containing all that is, ever was, and ever has been or ever could be. (I know, huh! Hard to get that through the noggin, isn't it?) That's ether for you!

Ether in balance feels: both grounded and aspirational at the same time. You feel connected to your earthly existence while fully realizing you are more than this physical form, and life is so much more than your material possessions, including your body. You have a connection to "higher" thinking and "higher" living and see fullness in and through all things.

Ether out of balance feels: as though living in this body and in this life warrants a good escape plan. You feel out of touch with reality and life and may tend toward wanting to "leave the body" in difficult situations. The body itself feels limiting and you might look unreasonably forward to the special day when you truly get to "go home." It's worth taking pause here to say this does doesn't need to be a morbid circumstance where you want to leave you life. Instead, it can simply be that you know there is more than what is present in the material world, and you have an affinity for returning to that free and spacious place.

Balancing practices for Ether:
- Walk in nature
- Garden and get dirty
- Go barefoot
- Practice yoga every day—challenge your body, your mind, your emotional capacity to sense and feel
- Practice maha pranayama (three-part Yogic breath with movement up and down the body) — You can find a guided tutorial for this at brittbsteele.com/PilgrimJewels
- Be with people—really be seen and be in your body whenever and however possible
- Make love
- Sit on the ground, outside with animals
- Put your belly on the earth
- Listen to music with rhythm, beats, and earthy tones
- Laugh
- Eat in community—organize potlucks, go to potlucks, plan parties where you eat with others and build your tribe
- Dance, particularly to music that includes drums
- Take drum lessons
- Eat seasonally and fresh and eat with your fingers (no utensils)

We are all made up of all five elements. No one element is superior to another. Paying attention to the elements can help us consciously bring more balance into our lives instead of having so many of those moments where we say, "I am just so _____ (stuck, overwhelmed, irritated, scattered, etc.) and then moving on as if we can't do anything about it.

62

The balance of recognizing your true nature and bringing your nature into alignment with what is happening all around you starts with two basic steps:

1. Know what element is at work in your life when things are going well for you, and

2. Know what element is at work when things in your life are not going well for you.

The more you recognize the power of nature within your own life and all five of your pancha maha koshas (great "bodies") that make up you, the more you realize how you can influence and direct the weather patterns within your own little world.

One Simple Practice:
Having read about the five elements, notice which element feels the most out of balance and identify one thing you can do to align yourself with nature today.

Touchstone #6: Be Breathed

You are the breath, the breather, the one being breathed.

Oh, this holy, holy breath. Breath is life. There is no way around it. And in order to live fully, clearly, and with vitality, one must have access to full, deep, and easeful breath. In so many ways, life is defined by the quality of our breathing. Some research suggests that we are allotted only a certain number of breaths in a lifetime. Other research shows us how the depth of the breath reflects our stress levels.

What is known for sure is that the first thing a human does upon arrival to this planet is to take one big inhale (before letting out that first "I have arrived" baby cry), and the last thing a human does before exiting the body at the end of life is to complete one's time here with one final exhale. In this way, life is one long story of breaths within breaths within breaths. On top of that, your breathing affects the way your body receives life's happenings and manages the ups and downs, joys, and traumas. Breathing is the single most important function of the body, as the health and proper function of all other systems and tissues in the body depends upon it.

When it comes to living your Yoga, I know of no faster and more effective way to ground and relax than to harness the power of breath by intelligently controlling this divine life process. When you are aware of, and in sacred symbiosis with, breath, you literally lengthen your days, increase vitality, become more resistant to illness, and you are naturally inspired.

Basic Breath Science:
This touchstone is about both the conscious practice of "breath training," as modern Yogis call it, or pranayama, as the ancient Yogis called it, as well as the recognition that upon bringing "breath" into your body, you are doing much more than just bringing richly oxygenated air into your body—if that were the case, simply by pumping richly oxygenated air into a recently deceased body you would be able to reawaken life. It's not that simple, for the breath contains some elements that science can prove,

but more significantly, it contains much, much more that science cannot prove.

13 benefits of awakening the breath
- Calms and quiets the mind
- Stabilizes the nervous system
- Balances the endocrine system and hormones
- Increases digestive power
- Improves absorption and assimilation of nutrients
- Strengthens immunity
- Balances right and left sides of the brain
- Regulates elimination
- Relieves depression and sadness
- Regenerates cells, tissues, and organs
- Brings luster to skin and eyes
- Reduces heart disease
- Increases overall strength and stamina

These benefits of pranayama are the obvious, scientifically vali-dated benefits of cultivating breath, directing breath, and assimi-lating breath in the body. But again, it isn't the "breath" that is nearly as important as the part about "being breathed."

What exactly is "being breathed?"
"Being breathed" is the touchstone that brings Yoga into your awareness and into your practice in any given moment. Being breathed is the recognition that you are not actually in control of this body or this life. For if you were, you would be able to control whether or not you breathe. Instead, if you choose to stop breathing, the course of events includes passing out, and starting to breathe again. That choice — to breathe or not to breathe — is taken out of your hands. It's outside of your control. Being Breathed goes back to Touchstone #2, Purify This Vessel, where you learned that through the process of breathing you are making way for life itself, for divinity to move in and through you and to animate you, or make you a channel for divine work, and to strengthen, balance, and regenerate your cells so you can do what you came here to do. When you do this, all is integrated. All is Yoga.

Yoga is not a science, although there are aspects of yoga that align gorgeously with science.

Yoga is not actually scientific, despite efforts of modern teaching to make it so, and although—as the 13 benefits above reveal—there are aspects of the ancient teachings that align gorgeously with scientific principles and research.

In addition to basic science, psychology has discovered that the breath reveals where you have unhealed wounding, stuffed losses, or harbored resentment. The breath requires freedom, in the body, to move in and though the entire body, and so consistent and ongoing breath practices can create freedom in the physical form, so you can feel it your energy, mental, and emotional bodies as well.

A few basic pranayama practices will allow you to command control over your breath and increase flow of vital life force or prana to your entire system or to individual specific locations in the body. In this way, you are consciously harnessing the rhythm and depth of the breath so that you may align what is occurring beneath your skin with consciously chosen harmonious rhythms outside of your body, born of nature itself.

I won't say much here, because you may not believe me and these practices cannot be passed on intellectually; they are experiential, so you'll have to try them for yourself. I will say this: Once you know breathing practices, and practice (get that?) breathing practices, regularly and with clear intention, it will unleash your latent power as a human being, able to do everything you have ever wanted to do which is aligned with universal laws.

By controlling your breath, you take control over your bodily functions, your mental activities, your emotional state, and your perspective on you, your life, and the world.

Early last century, one Yogi said:
"Prana, or life force, is in all forms of matter and yet is not matter at all. It is in the air, but it is not the air, nor one of its chemical

constituents. We breathe it in with air, and yet if the air did not contain it, we would die, even though we might be filled with air. It is taken up by our systems with oxygen, yet it is not the oxygen."

I know this can get heady, which is prohibitive in and of itself because you can't understand any of this through your brain; rather, it must be assimilated. That's just how Yoga is. However, this may help: The word spirit (think, "holy spirit") comes from the Latin root spiritus and it means, literally, "to breathe."

Amazing, isn't it?

You see, we are constantly inhaling air that is naturally charged with prana. Yogis learned thousands of years ago, not through double-blind scientific experimentation, but through personal practice and observation, that one's life force can be restored. They learned that the vitality in your body can be cultivated, directed, stored, and drawn upon when needed. I reckon this is how Gandhi, despite his limited caloric intake during much of the years when he was making the greatest impact in India, was able to be physically and mentally awake, productive, and clear. I reckon that Mother Teresa was tapping into the same thing—call it holy spirit, life force, or prana—and storing it in her body, so that well into her 80s she was eating very little, sleeping less than four hours a night, walking long distances in the hot sun, and serving her people.

Think of prana as "vitality," which in and of itself is pretty much an unknown formless entity, and it might make more sense. By practicing the three-part Yogic breath as well as a few other select pranayama practices, you translate breath (which carries the prana) into resources that you can cultivate, store, spend, and exhaust as you go throughout your days. The practice of self-study I spoke of in the beginning, called svadhyaya, becomes once again a very important part of this journey.

Try this:
Sit for a moment and let your mouth fall open.

Exhale and listen for the subtle sound of the breath.
Inhale and hear the subtle sound of the breath.
As you exhale, now add the sound "yh" to your exhale.
As you inhale, now add the sound "wh" to your inhale.
Do you hear what I hear? I offer that you are hearing a sound
that means in its literal translation "divine warrior," because divinity is unquestionable light and love, and to breathe in this way
you are practicing a mantra—a tool of the mind, if you will, that
will allow you to circle back again and again to being for yourself,
in and through yourself, and for others and the world, a sweet
warrior dedicated to love and light.

Like any brilliance, you must practice breathing, and consciously
practice the sweet surrender to "being breathed" to yield these
profound effects. Over time you will be able to easily access and
recognize the immediate and long-term benefits of these practices.

One Simple Practice:
Sit tall with your spine upright and your legs comfortable. Close
your eyes and breathe in and out of your nose. As you inhale, feel
the back of your crown reach skyward as you inhale the breath
up your body and root your bottom downward. As you exhale,
feel the spine continue to extend upward as your breath moves
down your body. Choose a length for these breaths that is long
enough for you to feel "full" on each inhale. Do this 13 times.

Touchstone #7: Rest and Reflect

Have you ever noticed how human beings have a way of working hard, playing hard, and resting only when forced to do so as a symptom of being sick or exhausted? Resting because you have to isn't the best nor most effective way to get the most of your resting time. When you are overtired, even extra hours of sleep will not rejuvenate you as much as regular moderate rest can. Just because you sleep six or more hours doesn't mean you are getting proper rest and recovery from your sleep. What you do before you go to bed and immediately upon rising has a huge influence on how effective your sleep is in restoring your health and hitting the vitality reset button.

Let's jump right in, shall we? Here are some of my favorite tips for before bed and immediately upon waking each day. I find that when I practice these things, my rest is deeper and I wake inspired and ready for the day.

Before bed:
- Massage warm oil on your feet (and then sleep in socks)
- Allow 15 minutes of silence before lights out
- Sit in quiet reflection/meditation for 10 minutes
- Allow one hour free of technology (including TV) before sleep
-

Upon awakening:
- Reflect
- Breathe
- Stretch
- Take it slow

To make the most of your rest time, it's worth knowing a few details about your body and how it relates to the rhythms of nature. Did you know that our bodies are aligned with the daily rhythms, much like the sun and the moon? We call these circadian rhythms, and to learn more about them you can observe and learn from the sun and the moon and transpose what you learn onto your life.

Think about this: When it is daylight, you naturally feel the pingala, or sunny side of life. When it is nice outside, you naturally experience more energy. It's not just you. It's natural. This is where and when you shine, penetrate, produce, and expand, just as the sun does. And then there is the ida, or quiet side of your life. This is where the body cycles into parasympathetic nervous system activity—the autonomic nervous system becomes dominant and all those wonderful things you don't need to think about (like moving food through the digestive tract, breathing, and keeping the heart beating) become of utmost priority in the land of physiology and functionality. In this way, intuition goes up and extroversion goes down.

Your body is always pulsing with the rhythms of nature, the seasons, daylight, and moonlight. Taking just a little bit of time to understand this and align with these powerful rhythms can mean the difference between living fully and merely existing in this life.

One of the most powerful ways to tap into your own need for rest is to notice how a child responds to lack of rest. We can all identify tired and cranky children, acting out based upon what their bodies are seeking. As adults, the only real difference is that you have learned to mask your need for rest with caffeine, convincing self-talk, override programming, and avoidance. The body simply requires downtime to maintain a strong immune system and to sustain personal resiliency, emotional regularity, and overall vitality. I know it sounds simple, but it can be a huge challenge. We have been taught to feel as though we need permission to rest, and those permission slips are hard to come by in today's world.

Turn down the busy.
This comes, ideally, in the midst of rest. It is where you exhale, release what you are holding (and more importantly, what is bound to be holding you), and you stay present to what is arising, while at the same time you do your best to stay completely relaxed. One of the most powerful ways to do this on the Yoga path is to practice what is called Yoga Nidra. This is where the body is completely relaxed while the mind is alert. In this way, you are able to notice what bubbles to the surface and provide space and

consciousness to it as it comes to your attention; because your mind is alert, you are able to bring it forth and do something useful with it. You can get a free Yoga Nidra recording on my website at BrittBSteele.com/PilgrimJewels

Honoring the moon's cycles is also a great way to set time aside to rest and reflect. One of the absolutely most powerful ways to tap into the rhythm of nature, and to find space and time to rest and reflect, is to use the full moon as a complete technology fast—no talking on the phone, no cell phone, no texting, no email, no social media. Then, use the new moon as a day of silence to usher in all the newness of personal expansion and possibility. New moon is a beautiful time to rest into the darkness, and to listen closely to your inner voice. Notice what is quiet and dark and wanting to be heard. You can do a moon svadhyaya practice for both the full and the new moon to gain insight and to align yourself with the power of the lunar cycle. Both full moon and new moon are great opportunities to offer yourself a full day of rest from talking, technology, eating, and even practicing asana. Full moon and new moon are both excellent days to do a 13-minute meditation practice if you don't have a regular meditation practice, or to do 108 minutes of silent observation and practice if you already meditate regularly.

If, like me, you teach yoga, I suggest you find a good moon salutation to teach your students and allow at least 13 minutes of savasana at the end of practice. You can find a guided 13-minute savasana practice on my website at BrittBSteele.com/PilgrimJewels.

These cycles are alive and well in our bodies, whether we acknowledge them or not. And when you honor them and recognize them (literally: re-cognize them) in your body and your life, you bring them to the forefront of your attention while they are present, resulting in more energy, more sourcing, and more effectiveness in and through all aspects of life.

When you rest properly, and when you take the time to reflect and create space for healing to happen naturally, cellularly, you recalibrate. Your cells are enforced with positivity and the integral wisdom of life. We are part and parcel of nature and there is no way to get around that. And if you avoid it, there is a point where balance will be regained, and there is a good chance it will be at the expense of your own health.

One Simple Practice:
Take the breath practice you did in Touchstone #6, Be Breathed, and do it again. This time, do it with an intention of opening a sort of energetic "drain" at the bottom of your body on the exhale, and imagine anything that feels depleting draining out of your whole being. Focus on your exhale and do this 13 times.

Touchstone #8: Nourish My Buddhi

What, pray tell, is your Buddhi?

Buddhi is higher mind: the "already awakened" aspect of mind, the doorway to inner wisdom. The word Buddhi itself comes from the root budh, which means "one who has awakened." Buddhi has the capacity within to rise up, to decide, judge, and make cognitive discriminations and differentiations if and when you are prepared to do so. Being prepared to do so means recognizing that you have choices, each moment of each day, and that when you want to determine the wiser of two courses of action, you have done your part to ensure the mind is functioning clearly and also trained yourself to accept the guidance of the Buddhi.

So, how do we train ourselves to accept the Buddhi's guidance? First, we need to pay attention to what we are and what we are not. Through the ancient lens of Yoga, you are not who you think you are. You are so much more, and so much less, all at the same time.

> **You are not who you think you are**
> **you are so much more**
> **and so much less**
> **all at the same time**

Through Yoga, you are made up of five "bodies" or layers of your being, from the subtle to the gross. Just as you explored the five elements (earth, water, fire, air, and ether) in and through all things, these five elements also live in your body or what we call pancha maha koshas—the five great veils or layers of which we are all made.

Here are the five pancha maha koshas:

Anamaya kosha:
This physical form is the most gross... the most obvious... and the noisiest of the five bodies. It is literally translated as the "modified food body."

Then, beyond the physical live the more subtle, less obvious four bodies or "sheaths."

Pranamaya kosha:
Also considered the "energy body," this is comprised of and accessed through the breath and its energetic contents.

Manamaya kosha:
This is the "mental body," which is much like an "operations manager": well-versed at giving orders, but still subject to getting caught up in delusions and emotional detours.

Vijnayamaya kosha:
Considered to be the body of knowing or wisdom, this body is adept at seeking higher practices, Truth, and conscious ways of being in the world.

Anandamaya kosha:
The body of "complete fullness," this is what ultimately guides us to find peace, joy, and bliss, simply by being. This is the most subtle and simultaneously the most penetrating of the five bodies.

So where does the buddhi fit in here? Directly related to the integration of the bodies... and rising up, up, up. In other words, it is about realizing that the body you usually refer to as "my body" is just a tiny little part of the big picture of "me"—and that as you go deeper and deeper on this journey, you want to default to the higher aspects of yourself, the wiser, more Truth seeking, and love-steeped part of you. And that, my friends, will tap you right into your very own buddhi.

So why nourish the Buddhi? The buddhi, in stark contrast to the mind, always has your best interests in mind. It may seem like a small distinction, but how many times in your life have you found yourself having made a decision, said yes when you wanted to say no, overcommitted to something, or walked away from an opportunity out of fear even though you really wanted to go for it?

That was your mind talking. Getting in the way. Getting all Bossy Pants on you and losing sight of the fact that you didn't come here to prove yourself to yourself or anyone else. You succumbed to peer pressure!

Buddhi is the one in you who is tapped in, tethered to something bigger than your imaginings, and always, always, always has your very best interests in mind

Have you ever noticed, I mean really noticed, the busyness of the conversation between your ears? Is the conversation life affirming? Supportive? Or is it manipulative? judgmental, pushy, and controlling? And does that voice stay between your ears and direct its language at you internally? Or do you have moments where that voice, good or bad, comes bursting forth, like a cat that dashes for the outdoors when the front door opens?

I remember when I was in my early years of study and one of my teachers said to me, "Your biggest barrier is your education." It took me quite some time to assimilate that and make sense of this observation. But in retrospect, I see that it is so true. My education, my ego's attachment to being smart, falling back on the suitcases stuffed full of what I learned and my constant pursuit to find a useful way to apply such "knowledge" in every sort of situation, dis-integrated me from the moment, intercepted my ability to be open to everything as it was presenting itself, and shrouded every new thing that came my way in some old-hat way of thinking.

Truth is, you want to nourish the buddhi. You want the buddhi to be the tie-breaker and the final decision-maker: If life is like a factory of things happening, being produced and moved through us on every breath, you want buddhi to be making the choices for the factory. Otherwise, the mind gets its instructions from the habitual patterns stored in memory bank, colored by the binding likes and dislikes and the ego's limited interpretation.

All of the practices, mindful steps, and conscious observances found in this book are here to nourish the buddhi.

**For you, my dear, are way more beautiful
than you even know
You actually are the buddhi
the one who is tapped in and knows
what is best for you**

One Simple Practice:
In your journal or in the margin of this book, write 13 things you know to be true about your highest self. What is hidden dormant within you that is totally ripe and ready to be part of your day-to-day living?

Touchstone #9 : Altar My Consciousness

Bring it all to the altar.

As a girl raised Catholic, I learned about the sacred. Sort of. I learned about the "altar" and found that it wasn't a place for kids (and especially not a suitable place for a little girl, for there was no such thing as an "altar girl"). I also learned that if I wanted to get to know the Lord, my options were limited. I could go to church on Sunday, maybe slip out of school on a Wednesday afternoon for a little extra, hit the confessional booth (which was far from fun, and always a little weird), or pray on my own—which I did quite well—when I wanted something or when I lost something.

I learned that God loved me when I was good, and not so much when I wasn't. I got a lot of mixed messages, and a lot of the time, I presumed that God looked like a young version of a crabby uncle I had and stood watching me, arms crossed, head shaking in disapproval.

Although I heard that I was a "child of God," I felt like Cinderella most of the time, and I never, ever learned that I was divine. Divine and me were never in the same room, let alone the same sentence.

Not until Yoga.

And when I realized that I was indeed divine—not just heard it and tossed it around in my head, but assimilated it into my whole being—I cried and cried and cried.

In the words of Rumi:

> **You are not a drop in the ocean**
> **You are the entire ocean in one drop**

Yoga itself means "to join together." It means to bring together that which appears to be different, separate, or unique from another and return it, once again, to its full-figured wholeness.

**Om puranamadah
purnamidam
purnaat
purnam udachyate
purnasya
purnama adaaya
purnamevaava shishyate**

This means something like, "From fullness all things come, to fullness all things return. Never was there a time, is there a time, or will there be a time when fullness is not present and available, here and now."

Understanding the jargon and construct that comes with living your yoga every single day isn't a practice in memorization. It is truly a cognitive shift—a shift from how most of us were raised to view ourselves, others, the world, and God to the way Yoga sees ourselves, others, the world, and God. It is not about fitting what you are hearing into categories you already hold in understanding, for yoga cannot be boxed or categorized; for if you define it as "this," then it cannot be "that," and therefore you will lose the Yoga altogether.

**This living your yoga
every single day
is an alteration to the fabric of your entire being
It is an alteration to your consciousness**

And the best place to do this? Why, at the altar of course. Figuratively and literally.

These two words, altar and alter, go hand in hand on this journey. The first is a personally chosen, dedicated location where divine intervention and conversation takes place. The second is the process of shifting and changing in character or composition in a potentially small yet significant way. Yoga "yokes" these words together, providing a space to allow for transformation of your perceptions and inferences from the ways in which you were raised that don't really work in the holy scheme of things to an inclusive, light-centered perspective that allows for all of life to be revered, respected, and redirected toward light again and again on the conscious path.

In the ancient teachings, there are five ways we do this. These are what I will refer to as the pancha maha yajnas (pronounced YUGH-yahs), or the five great devotional "sacrifices." Why are they called sacrifices? Because what is being sacrificed is one's personal likes and dislikes in favor of drawing one's attention and directing one's life force to not what is personal, but what is interconnected and affects the big picture of life. Let's unfold what I mean by "devotional." When I use this term I am referring to observing what one does through the lens of love, loyalty, and enthusiasm. It is offering yourself completely to these qualities, so that you are marinating in them as you go through life.

These five devotions are listed in no particular order, which is important, because the practice of any one of these devotions does not take the place of another. Each is full and complete in and of itself.

~Daily Devotions ~
Ishvara (the one you worship)
Ancestors and family
Teachers and revered teachings
Fellow humans
Plants, animals and the environment

Ishvara, the one you worship:
Deva yajna is cultivating devotion with an understanding that all creation is a manifestation of divinity and expressing your gratitude for all that is given to you. It is offering daily worship to the Ultimate Giver as a way to humbly lay down the ego and recognize that you are not, in fact, the author, of anything. There is a force greater than you that animates your every move, your every breath.

Our ancestors and families:

Pitr yajna is the reverential bonding with parents, grandparents, and ancestors—even our forefathers—and the fostering of family values for the unity and well-being of the family. This yajna is about caring for your parents and elders and performing practices of gratitude for your ancestors' sacrifices and offerings that have allowed you to be alive and well, living life however you do today. It also includes upholding certain values and traditions handed down to you by your ancestors and passing these on to your children and future generations. (I'm talking about the meaningful ones.) This is also about caring for your parents, being tolerant of their challenges and cultural isolation and loving them as you love the One responsible for all of creation.

Our teachers and the revered teachings:

Brahma yajna is your mindful contribution to preserve love as a predominant culture. You do this through inclusion, sacred scriptures (of any tradition that touches you), your highest teachers and leaders, and anyone at all who has "raised you up." The take-home message of this practice is this: Never miss an opportunity to share your gratitude to your teachers and for your teachings in word, action, and deed.

Fellows of Humanity:

Manushya yajna is service to humanity with the attitude of serving the Divine source of all that is. Seeing divinity in everyone and serving people is the highest form of service. In such a form of service, there is only gratitude toward every person in every moment for giving you an opportunity *to serve*. Service is being sensitive to the needs of your fellow human beings, sharing and caring for them. As individuals, corporate entities, or collective bodies, you care and express that caring. You share your knowledge, resources, and time, and you also take quiet moments to wish goodwill on others.

Plants, animals, and the environment:

Bhuta yajna is appreciating all creation as Ishwara, preserving and living in conformity with the laws of nature, and worshipping animals, plants, trees, forests, and all other forms of life as divine manifestations. Worship is considering nature and all forms of life as sacred and showing kindness and compassion to them. Both recognition and sensitivity are involved; by recognizing cosmic forces, you do not take anything for granted. Instead, you are sensitive to the environment and seek to understand and respect ecology as vital to the sacred preservation of life.

These are the five devotions. Altering one's consciousness is realizing that everything you do can be a devotion if you choose—everything for Ishvara—everything for the greater good. And everything in this entire life is an altar, for where is God not? The pancha maha yajnas remind you to lay down the ego and let go of the attachments you feel entitled to receive. They remind you that the life you have is here because you have chosen it, consciously or unconsciously. When you look to everything you do in life—for yourself, others, your teachers, your fellow humans, the plants, animals, and all sentient beings with whom you share this planet—you realize that everything is part and parcel of a huge magic kingdom and you are no greater nor less great than the next. In this way, we walk together in reverence.

But what about the altar itself? Your altar is as tiny as the corner of your room and as vast as the entire universe

Practically speaking, to build your altar you can look to these five devotions and choose a symbol to remind you of their value and pertinence to your life.

Here are some examples I have on my altar:

(Deva) The one you worship: I have Saraswati for beauty and learning, the Virgin Mary for my spiritual roots of Catholicism, and a stone goddess to remind me of the power of the divine feminine (if I'm going to leave a gender out of divinity, I've learned, it's her - so I make sure she is always included)

(Pitr) Ancestors and Family: I have a photo of my family—all six kids and then some, and a picture of my mom and dad's wedding—even though their marriage was rocky and lasted longer than it should have, it was perfectly imperfect and everything is as it should be—lest I forget that.

(Brahma) Teachers and Teaching: My rosary that my grandma made me out of sterling silver rosebuds, a photograph of my current teacher, and a mirror (enough said).

(Manushya) Fellows of Humanity: A piece of fabric I found on the street that belonged to someone somewhere, and frankincense and myrrh to remind me of the three kings and all those lowly peeps that didn't know they were as holy as the holiest back when baby Jesus was lying in that manger.

(Bhuta) Plants, Animals, and the Environment: A few stones that are amazing creations, a little hair from one of my critters, and a fresh flower, every day.

It seems a little witchy, I know. And I suppose it is. Part of the root of the word witch comes from "wise woman" and "wielding powers." I get that. It's part of Yoga just the same, and I'm all up for being a sorcerer of light. If this doesn't suit you or feels in conflict with your traditions, then just remember that nature is magnificent and gorgeous and divine—regardless of the name of the source. In this way, a beautiful postcard or a photograph that shows the wonder of nature, plants, and animals in its glory is fully devotional in and of itself.

Altering one's consciousness by using an altar as a space in one's home, or by using the entire universe as one's holy ground for transformation, does not matter. You can offer reverence for all things. Inhale and raise upon the breath the greatest honor you can awaken unto. And as you exhale, lay down all binding likes and dislikes. Do what needs to be done in service of divinity everywhere. The altar allows you to see your family, your own transgressions, and your imperfections as whole and worthy of reverence—as every step you've taken, not just the pretty ones, have led you to this point in your life. The altar allows you to acknowledge that your cultural roots may reveal evidence of dysfunction and even with this, you can tease your heart out of darkness while still staying devoted to your family and in love with all that you are and ever have been.

You are not here to change others, the world, nor God. That is not your job, nor is it even possible. In this way, yours is an inside job. Altar your consciousness by choosing to shift your internal lens and recognize that you are all that is beautiful and perfectly whole in all of your imperfections. It is this that you bring to the altar each morning, with flowers to your heart. And when you see yourself this way, so too will you see the world though this lens.

One Simple Practice:
Choose one item per devotion (a total of five items) to add to a place you find sacred. Call it your altar. It could be a window sill, a shelf, or a tiny table, somewhere you will see it every single day without effort. Choose things that remind you of each of the yaj-nas: the divine, your family/ancestry, a teacher/teaching, fellow human beings, and nature.

Touchstone #10: Symphonize My Heart

**The entire universe is made up of sound and silence.
So too are you.**

I recently heard a story about Gandhi that seems pertinent to this
touchstone. Now, I don't know how much of this is true, but the
point to the story remains the same. Here is how I heard it.
Gandhi was a wild child, a busy-brain sort of kid. He was always
thinking, talking, getting sidetracked and scattered. His caretaker,
a wise and holy man, recognized it was important to teach Gandhi how to focus. And so, he told Gandhi a story. A story about a
baby elephant and his trainer.

Here's the story:

Baby elephants are matched with their trainers before the elephants' birth. Elephants can live to be 60 or 70 years old if everything goes well, so trainers are young as well and are partnered
with their elephants for life. The average weight of a newborn
elephant is over 230 pounds, already twice the average weight of
the young elephant trainer.

One of the first training exercises when the elephants are very
young is to take them through an open-air market. As they walk
through, the trainer is constantly removing coconuts, sugarcane,
pineapples, bunches of bananas, and shiny items from his prodi-
gy's trunk. Every item the elephant is interested in, he grabs with
his trunk. Now this is no surprise to the trainer. He expects this to
occur. And he has a plan. He prepares the elephant to walk
through the market again, and this time, he gives the baby elephant a stick of bamboo to hold in his trunk. The elephant's ex-
citement to see the bananas, coconuts, and shiny temptations remains, but instead of reaching out and grabbing them with his
trunk, he simply dances a little happy dance with his bamboo
stick in his grip.

So, why did the caretaker tell Gandhi this story? Because the elephant's persistent, uncontrollable grabbing at anything interest-
ing, shiny, or pretty in his path is the epitome of Gandhi's (and
your) untrained mind.

This was likely the seed that was planted to grow for Gandhi, his one-word, easy-to-pronounce mantra that he used to control his mind for his entire life. (His mantra was Ram.)

What is a mantra?

The word mantra is made up of two roots: man and trah. There are a variety of definitions for these roots; one definition of man is "mind" and one definition of trah is "tool." So, a mantra is a tool used to control the mind and to lead us from mechanical to conscious thinking.

I know this is true, for when I have practiced mantra I have found that the vibration of sound reverberates in my mind and heart, and instead of thinking about what I need to do tomorrow, or how I am going to get that one thing that I have been avoiding done in time to fulfill my commitment, I find myself sweetly lost in the sound, be it Om Gung Ganapatayeh Namah, Saraswati Namah Stubhyam, or just Har, Har, Har. Any of these are equally powerful and teach me how to let go of what is holding me and what I am holding.

Sound is vibration. Before you even get to decide if you like a piece of music, or whether some sound is offensive or pleasing to you, every single cell in your entire body has already assimilated it and has either moved toward harmony or cacophony.

Using mantra to symphonize your heart with the universal rhythms that are natural, healing, vibratory, and holy is incredibly powerful. So often, human beings are split between two worlds: trained very young to smile and put on a happy face, while on the inside there is badgering going on, or a sense of feeling lost in a world of confusion and sadness. This is cacophony: a vibrational disconnect in how you experience the world from the inside and how you are sharing your life with the world on the outside. When we do not align these, our prana (life force) becomes dull and unintentional, and we find ourselves drawn to activities, people, conversations, media, and experiences that keep us dull, heavy, and stuck.

This vibrational path can be shifted. Redirected. The first intentional step is the most challenging; the simplest seed to begin this process of moving from cacophony to symphony is this: Hold space for what you are experiencing and for what you really, really want—both in the moment and as a long-term destination or objective—and then say to yourself, I really want (and fill in the blank with what you want in the moment). I really want that cup of coffee. I really want a second helping of dessert.

And then follow it with, "I choose" and follow that with what you know is in your best interest and will get you where you really, really want to be. So you might say, I really want that cup of coffee, but I choose to have hot water with lime and bitters. I really want that second piece of cake, and I choose to wait 45 minutes and see how I feel before deciding. In this way, you are not pretending you want something else. You are fully acknowledging it, holding space for it, and choosing what raises you up.

Say to yourself:
"I really want... [fill in the blank what isn't in your best interest].
and I choose... [fill in the blank what is in your best interest].

You can treat your mind like an unruly child. You can love it, hold a compassionate heart for it acting out (to a degree), and then redirect, redirect, redirect. See it for what it is. Release the "charge" of making it good or bad. These first steps are the most difficult, as your samskaras (personal impressions and habits) have carried you for some time from point A to point B on this path of life with little effort. In order to blaze a new trail, you have to step off into the weeds, and that's not always fun, but it is always worth it. You can do this. If you spend a tiny fraction of your energy making this shift in comparison to the amount of energy you have spent saying you want your life to be different, you've got this. Trust me, you've got this.

It is all about blazing new vibrational pathways

Here is where Sanskrit comes in, and why I love it so. Sure, you can have your mantra in English. But when you practice in

Sanksrit, every single sound syllable carries a vibration of goodness, alignment, Yoga, and light. The English language was developed to transact between humans. Sanskrit was developed to
communicate with the divine that lives in every human, at the
heart of their very being. Every single kara (sound syllable) is a
name for or a characteristic of God, and so you simply cannot
sound, sigh, chant, sing, practice japa (the repetition of mantra),
or listen to kirtan (community mantra in a call-and-response fashion) without praying. And praying in a way that is recalibrating
your heart with the entire symphony of the cosmos. This is just so
cool!

This is symphony. From cacophony to symphony.

I know this works. I really, really know this works.

Some time back, my husband had an accident on my horse, and I
seriously didn't know if I had lost him. Between the time I heard
screams for help coming from the area where my horse had been
with my husband and the trainer, and me running into the house
to call 911, I was realizing he was unconscious and I had no idea
if he had a pulse. The first thing I thought wasn't a thought. It
was a mantra I had been practicing—om namah shivayah—that
had been going through my mind and body for weeks. In that
moment, instead of spinning off into, Holy NO! What if he's
dead? What am I going to do? Did he have a heart attack? What
happened? Instead, I went, Om namah shivayah. om namah
shivayah. om namah shivayah. om namah shivayah. om namah
shivayah. om namah shivayah. om namah shivayah. om namah
shivayah. I slipped into the sounds that translate as, "In the name
of all that transforms beginnings, sustainings, and endings of all
things at all times into light and universal threads that connect all
things in all ways." And my mind went there over and over and
over again. I was able to split my attention between divinity and
the wholeness at the source of all things, and handling a very
stressful situation. I knew everything was all right (not just all
right), no matter what happened, and my heart was wide open,
and I felt peace as the container for all other emotions. My mind
was clear, and I did what needed to be done, moment by mo-

ment, breath by breath, from the 911 call to the ambulance ride, to the weeks of care that led to his full recovery. Nothing mattered and everything was sacred, all at once.

That is what symphonizing my heart looks like.

Now, it takes abhyasa (practice), no doubt. In the days leading up to life's surprises, be it a fender bender, a diagnosis, or a significant loss, life is happening all around you. When you have tools to control your mind when it wants to run off, you can bring your breath, thoughts, and emotions back into balance with all that is. Life is not only very doable (note: I did not say "manageable"), it is so very sweet.

Mantra organically involves the breath. And prana moves on the breath, carrying your thoughts, words, feelings, and emotions as it goes. So, if you can reprogram the breath, you can reprogram the way prana moves, and you can change everything.

What is Japa?

Japa in Sanskrit literally means "to mutter", and given that every sound symbol in the Sanskrit language is a name for the Divine, Japa is muttering the name of the Divine. Practically, it is the ongoing repetition of a mantra, over and over and over again. You chant while remaining conscious of the sound moving out of silence into its complete expression and resolving back into silence. You settle into a rhythm and repeat this mantra 12, 28, 54, or 108 times—or eventually you may chant a chosen mantra 100,000 times in order for every akshara (character or syllable) to awaken what is called mantra siddhi, the blessing of the mantra.

The practice of japa is a laya—a circle or a circuitry of energy. It is as though you are living within the sound, existing within the meaning of the mantra, while this sacred rhythm helps to reprogram all goings-on in the body and mind. In this way, you move away from chaos and into divine symbiosis... and you see the world as part of yourself, as an expression of your highest self.

In practicing mantra in this way, you go into this place of depth very consciously. You invoke your "devotee" as a conscious, light-seeking being. The chanter (you) resolves into the chant itself, and the result is an undeniable state of enchantment. It is very sweet. The vriti (sound produced) gets repeated again and again, and the ripples of that vriti go on and on long after the practice has finished.

That sacred structure sees you as a conduit between the microcosm and the macrocosm through the focus of shabdha pradhanam (sound predominance). This means that you are not focusing on the meaning of the words, but simply refining the sound, the phonetics, the relationship between sounds and silences and you resolve, without effort, into the vibration itself. You resolve back to sacred structure. You resolve into sacred symbiosis.

One Simple Practice:
Find a place out of concerning earshot of others. Take a comfortable seat and take three long deep breaths. Add om to your exhale for 13 breaths. This means you inhale deeply and then, upon the exhale, sound a full and rooted, resounding om throughout the entire exhale. Witness how it changes from the first to the 13th and notice how you change as a result of the om current moving through your body.

Touchstone #11: Awaken Through Asana

Yoga has so very little to do with yoga poses.

Here we are. Just around the bend from the last of the 12 touch-stones and realizing that Yoga is so much more than all of those fancy acrobatics we have seen on the internet and maybe even aspired to in our own practice. It is no coincidence that asana takes a seat this far along on the pilgrimage.

Yoga is so much more than what meets the mat.

You spend a great deal of time looking for what yoga is, and simply in the searching, you are missing the point: Yoga isn't actually something that you do. It is who you are.

The word asana is often loosely and somewhat flippantly described as "a seat" or a "pose." But, again, it is so much more than that.

Here are some definitions of asana that may suit you more completely.

The word asana means posture, but it also means:
state of being
reaching across
dwelling
abiding

Think about this. When you "take an asana" in yoga, or you move through a vinyasa (flow of asanas) on your mat, from one to the next to the next, you are dancing with your body parts, your breath, and your life. You are recognizing the state of being of each of the poses, such as "tree," "fish," "wheel," or "mountain." You are having a conversation with these poses and saying in and through your body that you both surrender yourself to the qualities of that entity and you are also offering reverence to those qualities.

Here is an example: Tree. What are the qualities of a tree? Stable? Rooted? Upward reaching? Transformational? One with nature? Patient? Mobile? Tall? Steadfast? As you practice tree pose, you are reaching across your separateness from the pose and realizing that all trees are you and that you are all trees. That you, too, are stable, rooted, upward reaching. That you, too, have the natural power to transform and to grow against gravity. That you are patient and can move and shift with the seasons of life and the winds of change. You can dwell in these possibilities and are not limited to your small, separate thinking. You are all that... and every other asana that ever was, ever could have been, is, and ever will be or could be. You are all that. And all that is abiding—built to last.

In this way, you are yoga. And you are Yoga.

And, still, you might really dig that you can do that fancy pose. That's cool. Dig it. And re-cognize that you are that cool pose, and you are so much more and so much less all at the same time.

I get it. We are on the 11th Touchstone and it's getting really deep here... Seriously deep. But it's time. You are deep. You are deeper than the deepest. So let's get on with it, shall we?

The next big piece about asana is that you must be very, very careful to not distract yourself from the reason yoga asanas ever came to be. The asanas have never been here (until very recently) to "manage low back pain" or "improve posture" or to "prepare you for eka pada chakrasana, one legged wheel pose." Not so much.

They came to be. They came to be, not to prepare us for doing something. They came to be to prepare us for doing nothing.

There's a story that might drive this home for you. You know Shiva? The God of Destruction, as he is so unfortunately known? (A little side note: I prefer to call him the God of Renovation.) Anyway, Shiva is known to be seriously powerful. The most powerful of warriors. Strong, destructive, transformative, and a little hot-headed. And he is known to be the one cosmic force in the universe not to be messed with. Ya know what his favorite asana is? His favorite "dwelling" or "state of being"? Sukhasana. Simple seated posture. Sukhasana!

Seriously. This warrior? He prefers to just sit there. No starting fires. No fighting big battles. No whipping his weapons around. But just sitting there in a simple seated criss-cross-apple-sauce pose.

That's it.

We came to asana to learn to sit.

To learn to sit so we can hear the voice of God within.

Sit. That's it.

Now, that may sound a little odd or impractical, but really the reason asanas were designed was not with a purpose to design something or choreograph something, but instead because those sanyasis (ancient Yogis) that were sitting in the caves meditating to their hearts' content were getting stiff and distracted by the aches and pains in their bodies. The reason that asanas came to be was purely out of a desire to diminish the distraction the body is known to present when it is in pain, or tired, or struggling. And so these asanas came to be to bring us to a state of ease and comfort so meditation or contemplation on God and all the good stuff could come more easily. The asanas came to help us "purify the vessel" so divine light would have an easy way in.

So, I'll say it again. Sit. That's it.

But you don't just sit around, do you? You are a mover and a shaker. You are constantly managing your to-do lists and all that needs to be done in your life. Times have indeed changed and none of us are sitting around meditating in caves.

So, your bodies can distract you, yes? So can your mind. Modern yoga practices have brought you to a place where you are wandering around between your ears so intently that you barely scratch the surface of your asana practice and find yourself thinking about techniques, choreographing, and planning that next big asana to master. All the while, the subtle body is just hanging out waiting for you to wake up and realize your power. And that can't happen when you are thinking all the time. It doesn't happen when you are reaching for this block or buckling that strap, concerning yourself with spiraling this bone, lifting that arch, tucking this or engaging that. In many ways, all of those fancy props and techniques and strategies become the distraction. Instead of meeting prana in your body, you get lost in a bunch of superficial garb and mental meanderings.

So, I'm going to break all the rules of modern yoga on this one. I'm going to suggest that you not attend to your biomechanics and your technique. Not at first, and maybe not at all. I am going to suggest that you not worry over whether you could hurt yourself or get injured when you are doing this asana or extending the spine like that or rotating that joint that way versus this way. Now, hang tight... I'll come back to the technique and safety of the practice—but I offer that it is secondary. Secondary to this:

The three precepts of practice, as I've learned from my teacher, are as follows:

Free, easy breath
Long, neutral spine
Relaxed body

What if... What if... in every single practice, you circulated your attention and your energy in and through these three precepts before and while moving through your poses?

Let me show you what I mean:

Free, easy breath:
Ask yourself, "Is my breath able to move freely through my entire body? Can I feel the impact of breath moving out to my appendages? Can I sense the ease of the inhale? The exhale? The

transition from the in breath to the out breath, and back again, from the out breath to the in breath?"

Long, neutral spine:
Now, I'm not talking about the neutral we know in biomechanics. Instead, try this: Think "offense." Now think "defense." Now think "neutral." I mean that kind of neutral. So when you go to offense, you lean in... you push forward. When you defend, you startle back and retract. In this way, life will offer you many (and I do mean many) opportunities to defend your position, or to offend. I offer that in every moment, in every movement, there is a blessed opportunity to stand in the sacred gray and find neutral. Where you are not revving up, nor backpedaling. You are not offending or attacking the pose, your partner, or the paper... and you are equally not defending your position or your people. No charge. No positive charge. No negative charge. Just "aaaaaahh-hhh." That is neutral. And that only happens when there is space. And space exists in the physical body when there is length.

Relaxed body:
In every moment, on every breath, with every single blink of an eye, step of a foot forward or backward... go for a steadfast, relaxed body. "Re-Lax." It is a laya again, a circuitry. It is a circle of returning again and again to a place of ease, relaxation, freedom, and spaciousness.

Practice your asana from this, and you will only need "technique," "alignment," and "biomechanical strategy" when you've practiced the three precepts and something shows up that you can't make sense of. You may still need and/or benefit from understanding and applying mechanical principles to your asana practice, but with the three precepts in practice, you will most likely discover this need earlier and remedy it more gracefully.

And, I offer that your risk and incidence of injury will decrease if you embody and adhere to these three precepts.

Oh, and then? Then you can take these three little wonders into your life... and watch how you shift.

Magic, Pilgrim. Pure magic.

One Simple Practice:
Find a place away from others and choose a 3-to-6-minute piece of music that you love and has uplifting lyrics. Let your body move to the music and feel yourself connect to the three precepts outlined in this touchstone. If you don't know them by heart as of yet, write them on a piece of paper and place them at the top of your mat before you start playing the song. Keep moving for the length of the song and watch how the three precepts affect the way you move and the way you feel.

Touchstone #12: Worship My Way h[OM]e

This is It. You are h[OM]e.

This is the last touchstone, and yet there are no grand fireworks or a celebratory ceremony to call this journey complete. It's not like that. It's like this. If you've made it this far, I say to you, "Om."

Om is the sound that is made of three parts that, upon being put together on the tongue, become one. Ah-OOh-Mm, and together they are om. Om is the nature of God in and through you. It is the beginning, the sustaining, and the ending. It is the trinity, the holy, the whole. It is the whole ocean—as Rumi says—in you, as one full and complete drop of water. And yet it is not the wave nor the drop that is imminent and transcendent; it is the water itself.

This is it. You are doing it. You have not been given gold. You have learned how to spin straw into gold. Wealth of spirit is therefore available to you wherever you are. No one can take that from you.

This will feel great and easy, for a while, and then life will get in the way, once again, and the benefit of this pilgrimage will wane. That is just how life is. That is how God is: lovingly requesting you to feel and follow your longing back to the h[om]e, again and again, and you raise up your devotee over and over again, until your devotee becomes your default. To "live your Yoga," it doesn't matter what you say. It matters what you do. And it doesn't matter to anyone else but you. To talk about it truly diminishes its power. By walking this pilgrimage, you have experienced moment by moment the ways you can raise your devotee up, and how your greatest obstacles are self-imposed. You have realized that behind every "can't" is a "won't" and you have reminded yourself who you are—at the center of your center—and that when dark and light are both present, light eventually, and always, prevails.

You are pure light, Pilgrim. Pure light.

You are the light you have been seeking.

Worship my way h[om]e. After all that, what exactly does that mean? It means that the one thing that distinguishes a spiritual life from a material life is pure consciousness. Consciousness is light. So pay attention, move with intention, and you will find that the light of your own being will show you the way h[om]e again and again.

One last story before we go. Imagine, if you will, a "master" walking through the forest. He picks up a stick to wield as an instrument exemplifying his mastery. He uses it however it best serves him. Then, he sets down the stick and walks on. Now, imagine this "master" walking through the forest. He picks up a stick to wield as an instrument exemplifying his mastery. He uses it however it best serves him and then he begins to set it down... and then he stops. He thinks, Wait, maybe I should keep this stick... It's a good stick. I shall carry it with me... just in case. He keeps walking, stick in hand. He walks and walks. Days turn to months, months to years. He thinks to himself, It is hard to remember my life without this stick. Could it be that this stick is what makes me masterful? What if I set it down? Would I crumble? Would I lose all that I have worked so hard to become? Would this journey be fruitless if I was not a master? Not with this stick?

You see, it's like this: One who carries the stick and wields it, then drops it, in mind and action, is a true master. One who carries the stick, and leans on it, has turned the same stick, the same instrument of mastery, into a masterful crutch.

I get that you are still learning how to use a lot of these touchstones as tools, and that some of you have practiced for years before this time, and have found sweet mastery with some, while feeling a bit novice when rubbing up against others. That's okay. No problem at all. Just circle back to svadhyaya and recognize what is really true for you. Which of these touchstones have you mastered? And which have you barely even handled? Is it time to put down some of the ones that are hindering you? Upon which you have become reliant?

Here are a few questions for you:
Do you have an asana practice or does your asana practice have you?
Do you have a morning cup of coffee or does your coffee have you?
Do you have a healthy eating plan or does eating healthy have you?

There are many more you can ask yourself; the list can go on and on... you choose which aspect/practice/habit/samskara/role/hat you wear, etc. that you would like to put into this phrase.

I encourage you to delve deeply into this one. It sets the foundation for your next steps.

Here is what it comes down to: At some point, the things that have been your greatest assets, your greatest teachers, your greatest guides and gurus, will hold you back. If you can only function with a certain type of morning ritual or food in your tummy, Pilgrim, it's time you rub yourself seriously up against some of the other touchstones.

It's just like the Yogi monk in the ashram. He can live there for 40 years, learn every puja, perform every ceremony, know every sutra, sloka, and stotram by heart, and at some point he has to let all of them go to reveal his level of assimilation of sacred knowledge. Those things, as sacred as they are, are like swim floaties. And you know what the important question is: Can you swim?

Eventually you drop everything
First, the teacher
Then, the teachings
And finally, the divine

Then, you are h[OM]e

One Simple Practice:

Make a list of the 12 touchstones in your journal. Read them one at a time and close your eyes after each one. Recall and embody the blessing the touchstone has revealed to you. Bring the touchstone and all that it offers, as a means of living your Yoga, into your heart. If you find the touchstone feels incomplete or unfamiliar, simply open your eyes and place a heart next to it on the list. Proceed to the next touchstone. Upon completing this practice, look back at your list and notice which ones have a heart next to them. Return to those touchstones and flip through the pages for a reminder, and then repeat the practice of closing your eyes and recalling and embody the blessing of that specific touchstone, awakening the fullness within each touchstone. After finishing all 12, sit quietly with your hands at your heart and ask yourself, What now... Dear One? Listen. Listen deeply. And continue with your listening as you enter into your day.

This, Pilgrim, is living your yoga every single day.

Completing the Journey

The end is actually the beginning. (But you knew that.)

Congratulations. As you have discovered, Pilgrim: Living Your Yoga Every Single Day is a journey. It is not mental acrobatics but a rich and robust daily sadhana (spiritual practice) that allows you to tap into your own brilliance and to live life from a foundation of wholeness, where everything that happens, within and without, is somehow full and complete and enough as is—no exceptions. Every person, word, experience is laced with potential. When we rub up against anything and everything in life, as life will have it, we continue to reveal Truth when we are open to its presence.

We've spent our time exploring 12 touchstones, but even this has its limitations. My hope is that you have begun to recognize everything as touchstone, everything as teacher and teaching. Everything in life is delicately and deliberately positioned to help you rise.

Although this is the end of this book, and this particular journey, the reality is that the journey you will begin on your very next breath is more powerful than even this pilgrimage. For now you know what it is to be a master, and you know that the master can drop everything. Eventually, even the teacher and the teachings themselves may be dropped. The last tool you shall drop is your belief in the divine... because it need not be validated to be true. The second to the last tool you shall drop is your teacher... because you need not believe in him/her in order for him to be an instrument wielding Truth.

And, now is now. So, let's both end and begin with this: Let nature take its course. Be in the breath. In the moment. Follow your practice, however small it may seem. Be willing to be aware... intuitive... and be willing to keep walking in this meaningful, integrated way. Yoga is what you will find when you follow your breath, your heart, and your dharma. Follow your heart. You cannot bypass the heart.

And as far as your mat practice goes? If you cry on the mat, per-rrrrfect. If you rawk the house on your mat, perrrrrrfect. If you journal on the mat, perrrrrfect. If you do good on the mat, per-rrrrfect. If you do nothing on the mat, perrrrrrrfect! If you don't even get to the mat, perrrrrrrfect!

But stay conscious, my friend. Know you are so much more than you could ever, ever imagine and trust this divine pilgrimage on which you walk. Trust that which is worthy of your whole, holy Trust. Just keep rubbing up against these touchstones. And you will find the way to pure being.

Be Yoga.
Be Nourishment.
Be Nature.
Be Love

What shall you do now with this one, holy life?

Go forth, and light this holy world on fire with love.

A Little More Love

I have more love for you, and there are a couple of different ways you can access it.

First, each year, mid-September, I guide seekers, just like you, on a virtual pilgrimage, with this book as the guidebook. We have weekly calls, daily inspiration, and a "jewel box" filled with the all you need to bring more light, vitality, and integration of spirit into your life.

If you'd like to learn more about how you can journey with us, visit BrittBSteele.com/Pilgrim

Another option, if you prefer to journey solo, is to follow the link below and you will gain access to all of the support materials mentioned in this book.

BrittBSteele.com/PilgrimJewels

However we connect, I thank you for walking with me and I look forward to seeing you in the ethers.

Love,
Britt

PILGRIM

This is who I am.
Beneath masks and hats and history.
I am whole. Holy.
Enough as is.
And when this voice from deep within comes forth and speaks of
Truth, There is a knowing that bubbles, rises, and reveals each day,
Each moment as choice, not chore.
This revelation is laced with potential, possibility.
Illuminating me as Pilgrim. Pilgrim of light.
Shedding rays of curiosity and willingness to see
through the darkness,
to see into the likes of confusion, loss or sideway emotion.
To gracefully, softly, hold myself in sacred conversation.
And so I journey.
I journey inward, past the right and wrong of it, past the
illusion of limitation.
I know, in this limited body that I am *not* that.
For I am That.
All THAT.
And I know how to shine this mirror.
Pan for this gold. Mine this preciousness.
I know that all that wants to live through me must come through
the temple doors. I know that my offering, my service, my light,
shines through me from a source of brilliance much greater
than my softly lit imaginings.
And I know better than to exorcise the demons,
For the risk of driving out the angels is much too great to bear in
one holy life. I walk barefoot, toes spread, soul upon this earth,
touching and being
the healer, the healed, the healing.
The breath, the breather, the one being breathed.
I stand in this body tall, rooted, upward reaching,
Blooming forth and bestowing flower,
Then fruit, then seed to soil.
I am divine abalone dream
Turning head & catching breath.
I laugh. Oh, how I laugh,
As I source my body, my bones, my blood as bread, as dancer,
As slave for to all who want a slave.
I need not tell you, but I will,
That this whisper come from a source beyond, a voice beyond,
extraterrestrial, intracellular.
And I hear you.
I see you
I am you
And I thank you

About the Author

Britt B Steele is described as a love preacher, truth seeker, and a thought leader in the yoga industry. She is a yoga teacher, and yet to call her so is a grand understatement, for Britt uses yoga on the mat as the vehicle to guide others to see and embrace their innate brilliance.

Britt was born in 1970 in St. Cloud, Minnesota and spent her formative years living on an 80 acre farm in central Minnesota.

She attended undergraduate school at Arizona State University, where she earned her BS in Exercise Science.

She coordinated and directed the Fitness Program at the University of Arizona, where she also received her Masters Degree in Public Health / Health Education.

She conducted mind/body research at the Arizona Cancer Center and continued on to teach at the University and Community College level, as well as provide counsel for institutions and medical facilities seeking to bring integrative medicine into allopathic environments.

In the 1990's, Britt found yoga as a healing modality in her own life, and quickly realized its power to not only change her physical health, but also greatly impact overall wellbeing. Britt began teaching yoga in 1994, and has taught and studied since that time.

Britt has lived and/or studied extensively in Southeast Asia, India, and Indonesia and has traveled internationally to bring the depths of yoga to modern day life wherever and however she is called, teaching and speaking.

Britt is married to Larry Steele, retired professional basketball player and former Portland Trail Blazer, and team member of the 1976-77 NBA Championship team.

Britt and her husband live at Deva Daaru YogaFarm, a small farm and yoga retreat center one hour west of Portland, Oregon. Britt and her husband built Deva Daaru to show others that yoga goes far beyond the yoga poses, and can be integrated into every aspect of life. At Deva Daaru, Britt facilitates yoga immersions, yoga teacher trainings, and retreats. Her life with her husband at Deva Daaru YogaFarm is, in part, the inspiration for *Pilgrim: Living Your Yoga Every Single Day* and the online 108 day program corresponding to this book. (More at BrittBSteele.com.)

Although Britt prefers the pace of the simple life in the country, she continues to teach in Portland, at her home and YogaFarm, and by request.

You can contact Britt directly at: britt@brittbsteele.com and follow her as brittbsteele on most social media platforms.

BrittBSteele.com

Made in the USA
Middletown, DE
04 August 2016